MANAGING CORPORATE DESIGN

MANAGING CORPORATE DESIGN

Best Practices
for In-House
Graphic Design
Departments

Peter L. Phillips

ALLWORTH PRESS
NEW YORK

Allworth Press books may be purchased in bulk at special discounts for sales promotion, corporate gifts, fund-raising, or educational purposes. Special editions can also be created to specifications. For details, contact the Special Sales Department, Allworth Press, 307 West 36th Street, 11th Floor, New York, NY 10018 or info@skyhorsepublishing.com.

15 14 13 12 11   5 4 3 2 1

Published by Allworth Press, an imprint of Skyhorse Publishing, Inc. 307 West 36th Street, 11th Floor, New York, NY 10018.

Allworth Press® is a registered trademark of Skyhorse Publishing, Inc.®, a Delaware corporation.

www.allworth.com

Cover design by Mary Belibasakis

Library of Congress Cataloging-in-Publication Data is available on file.

Print ISBN: 978-1-62153-459-4

Ebook ISBN: 978-1-62153-471-6

Printed in the United States of America

This book is dedicated to
Benjamin J. Phillips and Rebecca L. Phillips

Contents

Introduction

According to the latest online definition of the word "design" in the Merriam Webster Dictionary, design means: "to plan and make decisions about (something) that is being built or created; to create the plans, drawings, etc., that show how (something) will be made; to plan and make (something) for a specific use or purpose; to think of (something), such as a plan; to plan (something) in your mind."

The same dictionary defines "designer" as: "a person who plans how something new will look and be made; a person who creates and often produces a new product, style, etc."

It is also interesting to me that the term "design manager" seems to have no definition at all.

There are many people on this planet who call themselves "designers." Design has become a huge word covering a great deal of territory (see the reference above to *something)*! I have a friend who has a hobby of photographing signage he comes across during his frequent international business travel. His slide show contains (among hundreds of other types of designers) pizza designers, fingernail designers, dog grooming designers, employee benefits designers, curriculum designers, software designers, insurance designers, landscape designers (that specialize in mowing your lawn!), the child's play design center, party designers, floral designers, interior designers, package designers, industrial designers, and on and on. Of course, all of these folks are legitimately entitled to call themselves "designers."

When I was managing the graphic design function at Digital Equipment Corporation it was not unusual to get a phone call asking, "Is this the corporate design department?" I would reply, "Yes, it is." Then the caller would ask for the schematic drawings for the circuitry of a new microchip. Of course, the engineers who designed this circuitry were indeed "designers."

With all of these legitimate definitions of the word "design" it is understandable many people are somewhat confused when they hear the word "designer."

The design profession has also changed dramatically over the last twenty or more years. Technology has not only changed the way we approach design, but also added many new definitions of the term "design." At the same time the value of design to an enterprise is also becoming more respected.

This growing appreciation for graphic design in the corporate world is also responsible for a major shift in the perception of an in-house graphic design function. A great many corporations are just beginning to realize that an in-house graphic design department is far more than a "service function." They arc instead beginning to realize powerful graphic design can be a critical strategic resource for the enterprise, especially as competition has become more intense. However, many managers of in-house graphic design functions are a bit unsure about just how to make the shift from graphic services to a critical corporate strategic resource. The information in this book is intended to assist the in-house graphic design department manager make the appropriate transition from service provider to strategic partner.

Over the last few years of consulting with in-house graphic design departments and conducting workshops for these groups, I have noted that most groups tend to have many of the same questions. I tallied all of these inputs and developed a list of the top issues in-house corporate groups are facing currently. It has been remarkable how many of the following show up during each intake session!

In order of how frequently each issue has shown up, these are the top ten:

1. How do we move from being a drop-in service provider to a strategic partner?
2. How do we get enough time to execute projects properly?
3. Many internal groups go around us and use external resources instead? What can we do about this?

4. Design is not perceived as a core business competency in our company. How can we change this?
5. Our budgets for projects are minimal. How do we convince the company to give us adequate funding for major projects?
6. Projects come in at the last minutes and internal clients want a fast turnaround. How can we get involved earlier in the process? How do we prioritize projects?
7. Internal clients often hand us a brief telling us exactly what they want us to do—and how to do it! How do we convince them to change this practice?
8. We are basically understaffed to handle the ever increasing workload, but management doesn't want to increase the size of our staff. What options do we have to obtain more staff help?
9. We are largely perceived as a necessary support function, but not really credible as business strategists. We are not even involved in presenting our design solutions for final approval!
10. What techniques can we use to demonstrate our creative ability and skills more effectively

Well, there you have it! These seem to be the most common issues keeping in-house corporate graphic design managers, worldwide, up at night. My intention in writing this book is to tackle all of these questions (and a few more) head-on.

Just to be very clear, this book has been developed for *graphic designers* working in an in-house corporate setting. If you are an employee benefits program designer, you will probably not find this book very helpful. The book is not intended to teach anyone how to *do* graphic design; rather the intent is to help people *manage* the graphic design function in a corporate environment.

Acknowledgements

It is important to me to give credit to those people who have encouraged, trained, and mentored me over the decades.

I believe the most important people were my parents, who recognized very early on that I had a strong aptitude for the arts. They enrolled me in an art school when I was only ten years old. Mrs. Brown, my teacher, was the first to help me realize that "art" was much more than drawing well. She also said that art and design are two different things. I will be forever indebted to the late Mrs. Brown for her patience and encouragement at such an early age.

Later, I had the privilege of studying graphic design with people such as Paul Zalanski, Jerry Rojo, Bob Corrigan, Don Murry, and Professor Frank Ballard, a man who taught me more about design and life in the design profession than any other person I have ever known.

In the corporate world, I was fortunate to have many mentors who were non-designers, but who helped me understand the role of design in business. These people include Art Kiernan, Peter Jancourtz, John Dickman, John Babington, Dick Berube, John Sims, David Truslow, Mike Maginn, Bob Lee, Robin Aslin, James Manderson, Hein Becht, Josh Cohen, Paul Jaeger, Dick Pienkos, D.W. Johnson, Jim Speedlin, Coleman Mockler, Karl Speak, and especially Professor Stephen A. Greyser of the Harvard Business School, a collaborator, mentor, teacher, and friend.

Over the years, I have also had the privilege of knowing and collaborating with a very large number of design management professionals. Through discussion and often heated debate, these people have helped me clarify my thinking about design and the management of design. There are so many that it would be folly to try to list and thank them all, but a few are particularly critical to acknowledge here: Wally Olins, Tony Key, Jeremy Rewes-Davies, Rodney Fitch, Rick Marciniak, Peter Fallon, Fred Martins, Jim Aggazi, Yolanda Launder, Bonnie Briggs, Jon Craine, Steven Conlon, Bill Hannon, Roz Goldfarb, Fennemiek Gommer, Peter Gorb, James Hansen, Mark Oldach, Tony Parisi, John Tyson, Raymond Turner, Peter Trussler, Dieter Rams, Gary van Deursen, Rob Wallace, Stanley Church, Soren Peterson, and the late Earl Powell, former president of the Design Management Institute.

There are so many more, but space does not permit me to list another hundred or so names! I am also grateful to all the participants who have attended my seminars and lectures. I always learn from these students.

Finally, I would like to thank my children, Benjamin and Rebecca, who have had to put up with my often hectic schedules and deadlines, but always understood and maintained their belief in what I have been trying to do as a design professional.

CHAPTER 1

Design Management

For most of my career, I encountered puzzled looks when I would answer the question, "And what do you do?" by saying, "I am a design manager." The usual response was, "What on earth is that?" For those of you who are design managers, or who aspire to become one, it seems essential that we figure out an understandable response to the question, "Just what is a design manager?"

In my seminar, "Managing Design for Strategic Advantage," I ask participants to explain what a design manager is. Invariably, there are as many answers as there are participants. Design managers often have a difficult time explaining their role in an enterprise, even to other design managers! Is it any wonder that non-design business managers don't understand our role either? If we truly want to become a core strategic business partner, then we must learn to clearly articulate our particular role in the business.

Earl N. Powell, former president of the Design Management Institute, tackled this issue in an article entitled, "Developing a Framework for Design Management," in the *Design Management Journal.* Earl clearly and succinctly expressed not only my beliefs, but also the beliefs of many other design managers, in this article. In fact, I decided to use this article in my seminar as "pre-work reading" for participants. With Earl's permission, I am including the text of the article here.

DEVELOPING A FRAMEWORK FOR DESIGN MANAGEMENT[1] —EARL POWELL

Since the early eighties, when I was a practicing design manager, I have often thought about how best to describe what it is I do. How does one define design management, understand its objectives, and establish a framework for the knowledge, skills, and attitudes essential to its success? Writing this article has given me an opportunity to sort through the bits and pieces strewn about my office, and to recollect discussions I've had during almost twenty years of design management.

We've talked about the title itself—is it design management, or is it managing design? We've considered the context in which it happens, whether that is fashion design, machine-tool design, or graphic design. I've participated in endless discussions of the role of the design manager as design group manager, or as individual designer managing a design project. Lately, there's been considerable attention paid to the objectives and benefit of the design manager as a partner or key player in the evolving vision and strategy of an organization—and to design working as a competitive weapon.

In a discussion with some design managers and educators in London, I realized that the Institute is doing all of this work to facilitate managing for design—a process of visual reasoning and decision making. This profession that we are striving to understand, develop, and support manages and shapes the context in which design can be most effective. And there are two sides to achieving this: First, the greater context—the organization itself—must be aware of the power of design for competitive advantage; and second, the professional responsible for the design group must be a leader with a core set of knowledge, skills, and attitudes.

I remember a meeting in the late eighties of the Institute's board of directors and board of advisors in which we attempted to agree on a definition for design management. I stress "attempted" because it is very hard to agree on a comprehensive definition of most important concepts without first establishing the context in which it applies. The definition we agreed on and which we believe could be applied to most situations was: *"the development, organization, planning, and control of resources for the user-centered aspects of effective products, communications, and environments."*

This definition does not work perfectly for all contexts, nor does it achieve much specificity. However, it does provide a general outline of the domain of design management.

As the world we experience becomes more complex and changing, the variety of our encounters with products and services increases and becomes more complicated. These encounters and experiences shape our thinking patterns, our behaviors, and even our language. Every encounter we have, whether it's seeing and smelling a flower, or filling a cup with freshly brewed coffee, begins with perception. The primary goal of design is to shape perceptions and therefore experiences of products and services. Thus, the goal of design management is to ensure that an organization uses a design resource effectively to achieve its objectives.

One of the key challenges businesses have faced in the last decade has been to get "close to the customer." Those that have succeeded in meeting this imperative have charged design with the responsibility of shaping perceptions of the organization itself, as well as its products and services. As the pace of change accelerates, design managers are further challenged to learn more about managing their groups, and about operating the enterprise.

Outlining precisely the knowledge, skills, and attitudes that provide an effective platform for the design manager to succeed depends equally on the context in which those skills are to be used. However, for both the corporation and the consultant design manager, managing for design means creating a context in which design can fully participate in all decisions that will shape the points of contact with, or the perceptions of, customers.

In my opinion, there are six categories of knowledge, skills, and attitudes that make up an essential core for the successful manager of design. These six areas overlap and share many qualities; they are only keys to rich domains of information and requisite actions. Three of them are intangible, qualitative, and softer; the other group tends to be pragmatic, tangible, and more measurable. The first group includes *purpose, people,* and *presence*; the second includes *process, project,* and *practice.* And each of these categories has its champions and its chroniclers, some of which I'll list in the following pages.

PURPOSE: *PURPOSE IS THE FUEL OF LIFE, GIVING BOTH ENERGY AND DIRECTION.*

For good reason, we always admire an individual or an organization with a clear sense of purpose. Their purpose gives them an energy and output that keeps them ahead of the pack. They seem to have most of the answers first; momentum propels them forward. Purpose appears frequently in discussions about leadership.

The design manager needs to have a clear sense of individual purpose. As well, this person must shape the purpose of the group he or she is managing, and ensure that this purpose meshes with that of the organization. Such a manager is valuable to the organization and prized by his or her group. When employees move from routine performance in completing their assignments to stellar performance that goes beyond those assignments, they have moved from being managed to being led. Sound management is the bedrock of leadership, as well as crucial to any effective organization.

There is an old saying, "If you don't know where you're going, you won't know when you get there." I would add that without purpose, you won't know where, when, or how to start. Also, I would say that the design manager must be vigilant to ensure that all of his or her decisions work toward a chosen purpose. The design manager who aims the group toward achieving the highest possible levels of product function, without an equal emphasis on product appearance, may find the company's products lose market share to those with equal function and superior appearance. Similarly, a shift in emphasis toward function can easily occur on a development project that simply demands extra attention to function.

In any organization, there are many dimensions and layers of purpose, and each may respond to different sources. Sometimes, decisions are made as a result of internal politics rather than customer needs. The design manager needs to create a context in which purpose is dedicated to keeping development processes focused, efficient, and effective.

Kenneth R. Andrews's book *The Concept of Corporate Strategy* is a classic work that sees good management in terms of three key components. First, as an organization leader, the manager builds the infrastructure and processes that give a group of individuals an effective operating capacity. Second, the manager's leadership role is won through effective communication, respect, attitude, and vision. Third, as architect of group purpose, the manager shapes and continually enhances the direction, strategy, and purpose of the group. Andrews's book belongs in every design manager's library.

PEOPLE: *PEOPLE ARE THE BUILDING BLOCKS OF ORGANIZATIONS. THEIR ACTIONS AND DECISIONS DETERMINE THEIR FUTURE.*

The design manager's capacity to focus and motivate creativity is essential for effective results. He or she must continually clarify expectations by example and by the use of careful communication to bring the best efforts to the right task at the right time. Design managers need to be able to understand and empathize with their designers' individual talents, and match them with the needs of the organization. They must also continually build and reinforce the core values and capabilities of the group and its position in the organization.

As design managers nurture creative capacity within their own groups, they can benefit the organization as a whole by helping non-design managers learn how to facilitate creativity in their groups and in development teams. For example, one key to creative thinking is reserving judgment in the early development stages and allowing all ideas to be considered. Once non-design managers learn how effective this method is, they can set an example for their own groups. Thus the design manager can have a ripple effect throughout the organization.

PRESENCE: *THE UNWRITTEN DIMENSIONS OF AN ORGANIZATION THAT OPERATE INFORMALLY, YET HAVE A POWERFUL INFLUENCE ON DECISIONS AND HUMAN INTERACTIONS.*

There is a fundamental human need for stability, consistency, and meaning, and organizations are more effective when these traits are present. The culture of an organization forms to meet this need and is a process of establishing shared basic assumptions that are brought to bear on all decisions. Managers refer to this as the informal process of the organization. Often heard of as "the company way," this corporate culture consists of tacit knowledge and the acceptance of the organization's values and norms.

Understanding this corporate presence can reveal to the design manager key points for facilitating change, as well as formidable barriers to change. This is particularly important in attempting to infuse the organization with an attitude that respects and values design. Legend has it, for example, that during the early days of Apple Computer, Steve Jobs continually challenged his people to "make their computers insanely great for the individual." This became a shared value, an underlying assumption of the organization, and it helped to produce Apple's user-friendly products.

PROCESS: *THE COMPLEX PROCESS OF MOVING FROM CONCEPT TO MARKET DEMANDS CAREFUL THOUGHT AND BROAD EXPERTISE.*

Design is the only discipline that has the process of idea development at the core of its education program and practice. No other discipline focuses as deeply or broadly on the creation and evolution of ideas. The capacity of designers to take an idea through a development process, examining the evolving concept all along the way from multiple viewpoints, is unique and part of the design manager's contribution to organizational success.

PROJECT: *MANAGING OR WORKING ON A PROJECT TEAM IS MUCH MORE THAN JUST MEETING SCHEDULES.*

Here is where we learn about the norms and values of our organizations, where professional development occurs, and where most of the political battles are fought. Taking charge of or being a member of a project team on the one hand challenges the people skills of the design manager; on the other, it fits well with his or her skills of viewing problems from multiple viewpoints and solving them through the development process. These skills are fundamental and unique to a designer's education. Design managers need to help the members of their groups utilize this capacity in order to take on leadership roles on their respective project teams.

PRACTICE: *PRACTICE SUPPORTS THE DESIGN RESOURCE GROUP THROUGH THE DAY-TO-DAY OPERATIONS OF FINANCE, PERFORMANCE PLANNING, AND HUMAN RESOURCE DEVELOPMENT.*

Achieving a balance of all aspects of design management is important and making sure the practice issues are given sufficient attention is a particular challenge. I see practice as a kind of platform to support the design group. I can remember that as an artist I really preferred painting over doing inventory, stretching canvas, sending bills to the gallery, and all those other things that were the practical side of being an artist. Later, as a design manager, because I strongly believe in continuous learning and professional development, I remember attending budgeting meetings and fighting for as large a professional development budget as possible for my group. I didn't particularly enjoy the budgeting and financial side of design management, but it was great to give my group opportunities to develop professionally. Learning the concepts of budgeting and finance is important.

In the end, good practice by the design manager becomes transparent, or is simply there supporting the group without being noticed.

BRINGING IT ALL TOGETHER

If you were enrolled in a formal degree program in management, you would probably find a few differences from what I have mapped out here. For example, read "strategy" for "purpose," "culture" for "presence," and "operations management" for "practice." To me, the simplicity of these words goes straight to the heart of things. But no matter what we call these skills, I believe they provide the fundamental framework for managing for design. How you adapt this framework for managing to your unique set of experiences, and how they continue to contribute to this framework, are important to me and to the profession of design management.

How the Most Successful Design Managers Describe Design Management

Fortunately, over the years I have been able to develop a rather extensive network of colleagues in design management. A large part of this network was developed through more than thirty years of participation in the Design Management Institute. Others in my network I have met through both my corporate and consulting activities. Many of these people were asked to present their views in an article also published in the *Design Management Journal.*[2] Here are just a few relevant quotes from some of these managers.

Tim Bachman, Principal, Bachman Design Group: "Design management articulates simple explicit and implicit communications that mirror the organization's values. It nurtures individual contributions that accurately express and interpret the organization's business objectives. Design management is not a departmental or a supervisory role. It is a strategic resource and purposeful organizing process. Organizations that integrate design management as a continuously reformative activity within their culture easily survive competitive challenges and the subtle cultural and technological changes that cripple reactive organizations."

Torsten Dahlin, President, Swedish Industrial Design Foundation: "As a profession, design management strives to initiate and handle design strategies in boardroom decisions and to follow up with implementation and communication. Design management strives to create understanding and awareness among personnel at all levels that conscious actions in even the smallest decisions are the core of design management. Design management functions in all places and situations in which the organization, through its structure, products, and employees, makes decisions about customer experiences and product quality."

Lizbeth Dobbins, Former Manager of Corporate Branding and Identity, United States Postal Service: "Design is the ultimate vehicle to communicate intent. Penultimate design is the execution of leadership vision. I manage design strategically and tactically as a pure and essential element that supports our vision, which is in turn built upon our strategic plan. If the strategic plan changes, then our design work has to change along with the vision. The vision drives our design work. Design can crystallize senior management's thoughts and can help them move from the conceptual to the real world of implementation. I think that design management is visionary leadership."

Patrick Fricke, Former Manager of Graphic and Visual Interface Design, Design Resource Center, Eastman Kodak Company: "Effective design managers are linked with strategic marketing, as well as with engineering. Effective design management produces compelling value—tangible and intangible—for the company, *and the company knows it.* Effective design management contributes to the development of customer profiles and value propositions that drive commercialization as information that is translated into product form, color, texture, and interaction style. Excellent design practices influence corporate identity, affect day-to-day operations, and are consistent with the strategic goals of an organization. Expanding design management/leadership roles and extolling the value of design to the company are the subject of constant scrutiny internally, and a source of very stimulating conversations certainly. Are we there yet? Not necessarily. Is there progress? Absolutely."

Martin Gierke, Caterpillar, Inc.: "Design management can enhance the strategic goals of an organization through vision leadership—that is, with the help of 2D and 3D materials—thus providing a reflection of the organization's aspirations. Day-to-day operations can be enhanced through effective participation in the activities that give substance to those aspirations. Ultimately, the identity of the organization will be a function of the balance between the visionary and the practical. Design management, in particular, is well suited to help strike such a balance."

Tim Girvin, Principal, Tim Girvin Design, Inc.: "Design, from an etymological perspective, means 'scribing'—a gesture about how an organization expresses its ideology, culture, products, and services. These assets are carefully guided so that the message is consistent and clear in all forms of expression. This coherency of message builds strength in the facilitation of strategic organizational functions, such as marketing, sales, and operations. Although the word 'management' creates decidedly tactical associations, what most organizations crave is 'leadership,' which is the necessary complement to management. Leadership is inherently inspirational—defining the vision and pointing in the direction of possibilities."

Fennemiek Gommer, Former Partner SCAN Management Consultants: "Most organizations share a common goal: to be perceived as better than and different from their competitors. Design management could be described as visual perception management. It contributes to realizing strategic goals if it ensures that the organization's visual language is consistent, distinct, and relevant for all its internal and external stakeholders. Design management is responsible for the design, implementation, maintenance, and constant evaluation of all items that are part of the total brand experience, from the instruction leaflet to the serviceman's uniform. For perception to become reality, design management needs to be one of its creators."

Tetsuyuki Hirano, President, Hirano & Associates Inc.: "In ideal terms, design management is a holistic, long-term activity, encompassing all levels of corporate functions. In long-term relationships, products, communications, environments, and services can be treated as a system. We use the concepts of 'bridge' and 'network' to express this sense of connectivity in all its strategic power—that is, design functions across all corporate activities, as well as projects from start to finish. Embedding design in all development processes on a day-to-day basis helps companies evolve in response to new opportunities and unforeseen conditions in unstable markets."

Tim Larsen, President, Larsen Design + Interactive: "As companies have come to recognize the enormous power their visual representation possesses to communicate, motivate, and inspire, design management has become *asset* management. Effective asset management reduces costs and builds value. Implementing systems that ensure a company is consistently represented over time decreases marketing costs as impressions build on one another to create image quality. Beyond asset management, design management is about *attitude* management. It represents not just a company's state of affairs, but its state of mind as well. As a company struggles to differentiate itself in the marketplace, its attitude is often the only critical difference between it and its competitors. Warm, friendly, professional, edgy—each evokes an emotion that can be visually portrayed. Good design management understands an organization's personality and communicates its attributes. At its best, design management is design *leadership.* It respects the past while guiding the present with openness to the future."

Peter Trussler, Vice President, Corporate Design Group, Nortel: "Design management is defined principally from a business and customer context, and it starts with a well-defined value proposition that is strategic to the client, followed by clear statements of vision, mission, goals, strategies, and action plans that link to those of the client and its business. Design management is about ensuring that the energy of the organization is expended in programs that are essential and strategic. This is achieved when linkages between goals, strategies, plans, and processes have been clearly established and shared by design management. As a result, all employees in the organization can see the alignment of their work with high-level strategic priorities. Fundamental to achieving this level of organization and management maturity is the adoption of a management/leadership system spanning a wide range of elements, including organizational values, performance expectations, communications, and focus on external and internal customers, as well as constant monitoring of overall results. If the value proposition of the design organization is strongly associated with renewal, reinvention, and out-of-the-box thinking, it is essential that design management be active in the executive forums responsible for giving direction and determining investment in advanced product research."

Raymond Turner, Former Group Design Director, BAA PLC: "Design is critical to achieving corporate mission. This means using design to help provide customers with what they want in a way that adds value to our business. In practical terms, we do this by *defining* what customers and other stakeholders want, and then developing the mechanisms for *delivering* it."

Well, there you have it—leading design managers from every corner of the globe responding to the question, what is the definition of design management?

As you can see, these leading practitioners of design management can rarely agree on a specific definition. However, every one of them agrees that design management is a core part of corporate vision, business strategy, and competitive advantage. It is far more than "project management," or simply providing administrative leadership to a corporate function. It requires a thorough understanding of the company's business strategy, the state of the industry on an ongoing basis, knowing the customer as well as anyone in the company, and understanding how to make the company's products or services leaders in the category through visual means. Great design managers also know how to translate all of this to their design staffs in a clear and meaningful way.

It is also interesting to note that they all agree that design management is more about the *results* of design and the *outcomes* of design than it is about the *aesthetics* of design. The most successful design managers always hire the best design talent they can find. If you do this, it is not really necessary to see your role as a teacher of design to design staffs. Rather, it is to be sure these excellent designers clearly understand the problem to be solved, as well as the desired outcomes of the design project.

The collaborative design brief is the most effective way for the design manager to organize thinking, then communicate it to design staffs, as well as to the rest of the company . . .

Finally, the comments from these leading design managers demonstrate that these people are leaders in the design profession simply because they understand how to articulate the *value* of design and they know how to think *strategically* in a business environment.

So, What's My Answer to the Question, "What Do You Do?"

Earl Powell gives us some excellent food for thought about what design management should be all about. Although I used many variations, my standard answer to people who asked me what a design manager did was something like: "I am a strategic business partner in my company and a key player in shaping the vision and business strategy of the company by making the company and its products (or services) visible through design."

I also often said, "I am accountable for the visual manifestation of the company's business strategy as approved by the board of directors and ratified by the shareholders."

That used to draw some attention! In one instance I made that statement to the CEO of a company. He asked me to have lunch and discuss all of this further. We became good friends, and I started to get invited to meetings he called to discuss corporate business strategy!

CHAPTER 2

Design Managers Must Be Able to Speak the Language of Business

When I was a student studying graphic design at the University of Connecticut and UCLA, I was surrounded by other design students and professors of design. Of course we talked a great deal about design all the time. We were, after all, attempting to eventually become professional graphic designers.

We used what seemed to others to be a very strange language. We would use terms like grid systems, negative space, kerning, color palettes, widows and orphans, hanging punctuation, serif and san serif, Helvetica, Boldoni, Garamond, Bembo, Palatino, and hundreds of other font names. We had our own design language, and we all understood it.

What we were not really prepared for was that eventually when we got into a corporate environment, no one would have a clue as to just what we were talking about!

In school we often had to present our design solutions to the class. The class was really tough on wanting to know what our thinking was, what techniques we experimented with, and so on—the process of design.

In the corporate world no one cared about such stuff. Rather, the corporate types simply wanted to know the results of our work—not *how* we did it.

I know I struggled with this at first, primarily because I had never really been exposed to the language of corporate business. I would be asked many questions about ROI, roll-out costs, shelf life, etc. I quickly became aware I needed to become multilingual, as it were. I already new the language of design, now I had to learn the language of business.

Fortunately, my first corporate employer had funds available for individual professional development. I entered an extended program (five days a quarter over six quarters) at a major university in their business school. It was all basic stuff, but I began to learn a second language—the language of business. It was one of the best career decisions I ever made.

Words to Avoid in a Corporate Environment

I also learned there were a number of words that a design manager should never use. They are words that work against you.

The first of these is "art." When I began my career there were still Art Departments. There were Art Directors, Art Buyers, and we presented finished art for approval. The problem lies in the fact that art and design are two different things! An artist is free to create an image, either two-dimensional or three-dimensional, that represents the artist's view of the world. An artist may paint someone's portrait, and the subject may either "like it" or "not like it." So be it, beauty is in the eye of the beholder. The artist painted the portrait according to the way he or she saw the subject. The result was a representation of the artist's view.

Design, on the other hand, is a problem-solving discipline. As designers we are charged to solve a specific problem through visual means. It is not about how we personally view something, but rather about designing something that works to solve the problem. That is why we call it a design solution.

When non-design corporate business types hear the word "art," they immediately think of something that is highly subjective. You "like" it or do you not "like" it. I would venture to say every designer reading this has heard that "I don't like it" speech more than once.

Of course we use many techniques in our design work that are also used in art. But the point is we cannot use the word "art" effectively if we want to elevate "design" to a more strategic level. I felt so strongly over time about this that I banned the term "art" completely from my design functions. No more art directors, art buyers, etc., they became design directors, design buyers and so forth. We were never an Art Department; we were always a Strategic Design Function.

The second deadly word to avoid in a corporate setting is "service." I still constantly encounter "Creative Services Departments." If your intention is to elevate design to a core strategic business competency, then don't proclaim to the world that you are a "service." If you proudly announce that you are a "service" then you will be regarded as a "servant." Servants usually have masters.

Think about it. Everyone in the corporation provides a service. The CEO provides a service to the shareholders, board of directors, and even the employees. But the phone is not answered in the CEO's office as, "Hello, CEO Services!" Tell everyone you are a service, and that is the way you will be treated. Please avoid using the word.

Finally, avoid all "design speak." One senior manager once asked me, "Just what is this thing, negative space?" I tried to explain it to him and he just shook his head and said, "So, if there is nothing there, this is something brilliant?"

Communicating in Business Terms

As a consultant, I have worked with many corporate design groups who are striving to move away from being a service center and becoming regarded as a strategic partner. I often ask members of the group to provide a list of words that describe how they see themselves as graphic designers or graphic design managers. Then they are asked to indicate how they believe other non-designers in the company perceive them. The results have been fascinating!

With very few exceptions, the first list includes phrases like "creative," "miracle worker," "talented," "fast," "overworked," "underpaid," "not appreciated," and "lifesaver."

The second list always contains phrases such as "difficult," "slow," "well-meaning," "a bit weird," and the ever-popular "necessary evil."

What is always interesting to me is that in the more than fifteen years I have been doing this exercise with graphic design groups, there are always *two* lists. No one has ever said, "I only did one list because the way I perceive myself is exactly the way others perceive me." One brave designer had only one list, but she simply said, "I don't think non-designers really have any perception of me, or what I do, at all!"

But, graphic designers always report a disconnect. "I am rather wonderful, and I work miracles for the company, which are never appreciated. The company sees me as a necessary resource, yet they won't listen to me or give me enough time or money, and they don't ever include me early enough in the process."

What's going on? Why do graphic designers feel they are so misunderstood? Why are they not included early on in the process, and why aren't their opinions valued? The answer is really very simple.

Traditionally, graphic designers have no credibility as business savvy people because they only speak the language of design. As a result they aren't trusted enough to make critical business decisions. It's all about effective communications and the power of using the correct words in a business setting.

As I tell groups, "the others" are not at fault for this disconnect—"we" are. If there is a major difference between how we see ourselves and how we know others are seeing us, then *we are not communicating effectively.* It is up to graphic designers to change this dynamic. It will probably take some time. First we need to learn, or re-learn as the case may be, the language of business. We need to understand and acknowledge that we are not being understood and appreciated because we are focusing on design speak and not business speak.

CHAPTER 3

The Model

It seems like everyone who embarks on a career to teach "how-to" seminars has developed some kind of model to illustrate critical points. So that's what I have done as well. The following is meant to be a visual guide to the process, which I have found works effectively for designers and design managers who want to improve the perception of design, and the design function, in the corporate world.

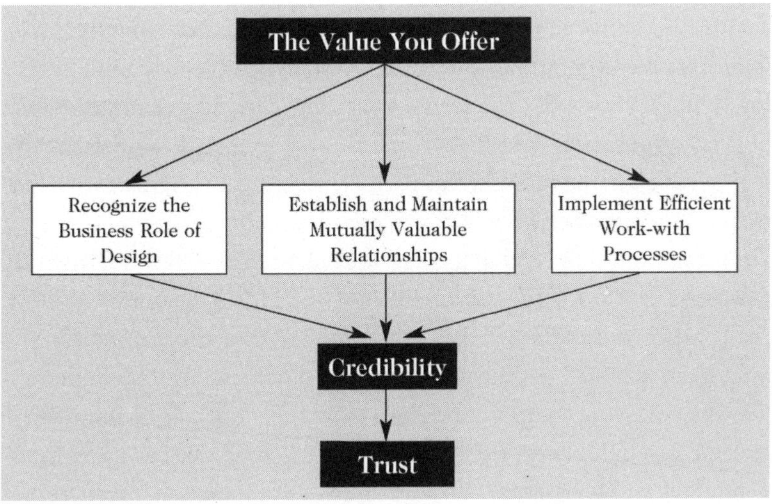

The Value You Offer

This is the most critical—and therefore the first—step in my model. If you don't understand why you are valuable, or why graphic design is valuable, then no one else will either. Many of us believe we know why we are valuable, but knowing it and *communicating* it effectively are two entirely different things. I would hasten to add that what we believe makes us valuable is not always what others believe is of real value. In the aforementioned exercise, with the two lists, the types of things people most often mention on the first list are not the things non-design corporate managers, particularly senior managers, are looking for. The items I routinely see on the first list are merely what senior non-design managers have come to expect from any employee. Being a person who gets work done on time, with very short time schedules, is a given to them. Staying within budget is also expected. Being very creative? Well, that's why they hired you in the first place! Being able to handle multiple projects at the same time? They do the same thing—every day. And the list goes on.

Graphic designers tend to list the "tactical" things they do everyday. There is seldom anything remotely "strategic" on the lists I see. To be truly valued, an equal partner in the process and a core strategic business competency, graphic designers must learn to speak the language of business and relate what they do to business results. If you want to be a co-owner and equal partner in the design brief process, for example, then you must communicate and demonstrate clearly that you are thinking strategically about the effect(s) of graphic design as a solution to the business problem. If your focus is entirely on aesthetics and tactics, you will never be perceived as a full partner. Rather you will be the "decorator," the "art service." Not that aesthetics and tactics will not play a significant role at the end of the day; they just can't be all you talk about.

When I say "the value you offer," just whom do I mean by "you"? In the context of this model, there are two. There is you personally, the individual who will be an equal partner in a process. And then, there is the collective you, the graphic design function as a whole. You want the graphic design function to be valued and respected as a critical component of the whole organization, and you also want to garner respect and trust as the manager of the graphic design process.

Why Am I Not Invited to Higher Level Strategy Meetings?

I often hear from graphic design managers that they are not included in higher level discussions about company business strategy. Since they do not usually have a seat at that development table, they are forced to become reactors.

With the growing importance of graphic design in the cluttered world marketplace, why wouldn't senior management invite the director of the graphic design function to participate in these planning meetings? It is simply because those senior managers have never valued graphic design as a core strategic competency that must have a voice in strategic business thinking. And, as already stated, this is a result of graphic designers having not been excellent communicators about their strategic business value in the first place.

I have consulted with a pretty large number of graphic design managers over the years who have felt the problem is hopeless. For twenty, thirty, or more years, graphic design has simply been a support service. It now seems improbable that graphic design can reposition itself. Please do not give up hope. You can make the transition. However the onus is on the design profession to actively demonstrate the value they can add to a corporation. This means a whole new way of communicating added value.

I recall one company in particular. The graphic design manager had been with the company nearly twenty-five years. The role of his graphic design group had been one of a support function this whole time. The company faced a great deal of new, global competition. Pricing of their goods and services was out of line with current business practice. The company's products had been of high quality, and fairly expensive to produce. Senior management was determined to find ways to become more competitive in the marketplace. These managers held frequent meetings to discuss ways to lower costs, yet still maintain the high quality image of their brand. It never crossed the minds of these senior managers that graphic design had any part in these discussions and therefore they never thought to consult with the graphic design manager.

Of course there were indeed ways in which graphic design could play a meaningful role in these discussions. Working with the graphic design manager, we produced a very compelling presentation for management.

We began by focusing on the problems the company was facing. We did this to be sure these managers understood that we, the graphic design team, truly understood strategic business dilemmas. We next outlined a series of actions graphic design could take to help solve the business problem. I won't list all these actions here, but some of the key points revolved around:

- Developing a new literature architecture that would result in producing fewer communications materials without losing the impact of the messaging (thus reducing expense of literature).
- Exploring simpler, less costly printing options.
- Revising time frames for development and production of communications materials to nearly eliminate "rush" charges. (The company had been paying enormous premiums for rush work, and most executives had not even been aware of these costs.)
- Eliminating certain items in the overall communications portfolio such as multiple newsletters for various product lines, and replacing them with one corporate newsletter which would be designed to accommodate the real world needs of each product line.
- Controlling all graphic design work from one source, the corporate graphic design group. Previously many product lines had been externally sourcing much of their graphic design work, and paying dearly for the privilege.

We were able to get a hearing for our presentation. Several senior managers were duly impressed. The most common comment heard throughout the presentation was, "We had no idea!" Nearly all of the recommendations made by graphic design were accepted, simply because there was a very strong *business* case made to approve these recommendations. Strategy, coupled with verifiable data and numbers, really does work. The company was facing some major obstacles in the marketplace, and finally graphic design took a proactive role in helping to overcome some of these obstacles. The graphic design manager was made part of the management

Paradoxical Leadership: A Journey with John Tyson

I have a good friend, John Tyson, whom I respect and admire greatly. John was trained as an industrial designer. Up until his retirement,

John was vice president of Nortel's (formerly Northern Telecom) Corporate Design Group. Yes, you are reading that correctly—vice president! Very few design managers ever become vice presidents of major corporations, but John Tyson did. He was able to get to this position because he understood how to effectively communicate the value of design.

In "Paradoxical Leadership: A Journey with John Tyson" by Artemis March—an article written for *Design Management Journal* some time ago, but certainly as relevant today as it was then—Artemis interviewed John Tyson, and included several quotes from John and others in his group about how they transformed the design function at (then) Northern Telecom. Artemis March is a consultant and educator who facilitates organizational transformation. She has directed dozens of field-based studies of companies for universities and business clients, including Chrysler Motors, AT&T, IBM, and Johnson & Johnson. Because the quotes from Artemis's article are so pertinent to what I am talking about in discovering and communicating the value of design, I have, with permission, excerpted portions of her article here.

Excerpt from *Design Management Journal*, article written by Artemis March:

PARADOXICAL LEADERSHIP[3]: A JOURNEY WITH JOHN TYSON

Northern Telecom's top management came to the conclusion that design was very underleveraged at Bell Northern Research (BNR) and its R&D subsidiary, and that the industrial design function needed to be reinvented if Northern was to achieve industry leadership in digital telecommunications. Wondering if John Tyson, then Vice President for Market Development in NT's transmission group, would be interested in taking on this challenge, the CEO told him, "I'm thinking of doing something with your old group—something big." Tyson's first reaction was, "It's probably not big enough."

Tyson's "old group" was Design Interpretive, the internal design group he had founded in 1973, a few years after he joined NT as its first industrial designer. But by 1983, he had opted out of design. As he explains it, "I got tired of talking about design and pushing. I decided to go to the other side and pull. On the other side, they don't value design. It's largely invisible."

Tyson's response to the CEO's "feeler" was vintage Tyson. Peter Trussler, who joined Tyson's Design Interpretive in its early days and is now director of the Corporate Design Group (CDG) which evolved from it, recalls that Tyson's confidence and free spirit were expressed as openly back then as they are now:

> When John first joined the company, they couldn't find a classification for him, so they labeled him a draftsman. He said, "Take that off or get yourself another designer. You don't understand where my value is. " . . . He would call a meeting with the president and think nothing of it, because he was concerned with the value of the meeting, not the protocol of hierarchy. He's not adverse to risk. He loves a challenge. He always has a very interesting way of coming at things. And he has always been that way. What you see is what you get. That's what's valued in this corporation. I think it reflects well on us that a person like that has been welcomed and valued, that he's not been chewed up and spat out. When there's a crisis, or a need for fresh ideas, or for someone to challenge things, I think a lot of people start wondering, "What's Tyson up to these days?"

Now, as you can see, John Tyson was not a shy, reactive design manager. John clearly understood that a major part of his role, and the first step to success, was to communicate clearly the value of design. Another portion of this article details how John Tyson approached the task of reinventing design at Northern Telecom.

> In the three months following his return to Design Interpretive, Tyson and his senior managers worked their way through a six-step "reset" of the design function. Tyson described the process as a journey in which "each step delivered the next one." The first step was the decision to reinvent the design function as a center of excellence. Once that decision was taken, the group knew it had to write a meaningful policy. Next, it changed the funding structure. The fourth step was defining the program, and that in turn drove the new organizational structures and processes. The final step is referred to by the group as "the pudding"—as in "the proof of the pudding is in the eating."
>
> One of the most frequently used words in the group's lexicon is "value." CDG people are constantly considering its meaning and how to translate it into product: What is value? What do users value? What is our value? How do we create value? They also talk a lot about accountability, and what it means for how they work together. This ongoing, evolving dialogue was generated and is nurtured by the core concept around which the reset evolved: that design was to be a center of excellence.

Although this concept cannot be pinned down in a precise mechanical way, Tyson's metaphorical language suggests that a center of excellence emerges from a dynamic, sometimes dialectical, process of the holistic convergence of accountability, value, and leadership. As he explains, "If you are a center of excellence, you're accountable." Accountability means that "we're accountable for the value we contribute to the corporation."

When he describes what assuming accountability for delivering value really means, it becomes clear that Tyson is a leader who thinks in paradoxical or dialectical terms. Disputing the view that accountability is about who's in control, he says, "To get control you have to give it away. We give it away. The value accrues to our partner. We invest in our partner." He observes that, by contrast, "most people operate as if value accrues to themselves. But the value of the work you do accrues to your partners, and to the user or chooser of the product."

The center of excellence concept is strongly underlined in CDG's new policy statement. In contrast to most book-size policies, Tyson and his managers wanted something very concise that would capture the spirit of the new organization. On the day the reset was announced . . . a carefully crafted one-page policy statement was given to the group's members. Signed by top management, the policy validates CDG's status as a corporate center for excellence, responsible for driving design excellence and continuity across all NT products. It acknowledges that the design group has signoff authority at all "gate reviews" in the new product introduction process, and that it is on a par with its partners in product marketing and product development in contributing to "new product definition, conceptualization, specification, and final design."

Tyson and his managers crafted a policy statement that concentrates on what CDG will *give* to the corporation. Design makes itself accountable for delivering a "leadership focus" and a "strategic driving force" for delivering "outstanding customer value . . . and product continuity" in order to "effectively contribute . . . to world industry leadership." There are no contingencies, no back-door escapes. Tyson describes the document as "a license that simply empowers you to be the best there is. It also says, "Today I am different than I was yesterday. Now I own this. I'm accountable for it." And that's why we had to change the name of the group [from Design Interpretive to the Corporate Design Group]." Although he had named the design group Design Interpretive, "it became evident in the journey that the name had to change. . . . What mattered was the metamorphosis."

I wanted to include this small excerpt from Artemis March's article on John Tyson because it describes how one design manager successfully communicated the value of design to his corporation. Each design group will need to develop its own plan for "resetting" perceptions within the organization. It is hard work, but worth the effort.

Accountability Versus Responsibility

I would like to call your attention to John Tyson's frequent use of the word "accountability." When you are truly accountable for something, that means your job, reputation, and credibility are on the line. You are accepting full *accountability* for your work. You are willing to step up to the plate. You are putting your career on the line.

On the other side is "responsibility." Responsibility is not quite the same as accountability. During my many years as a director of corporate design for several companies, I was accountable for the work and design solutions from my groups. If things didn't go well, I was the one called on the carpet. I was the one who could get canned. There were many folks in my design groups who were *responsible* to get certain things done. And I held them responsible. But as director of the function, senior management held me *accountable.* I was the one with a job on the line.

Once again, language means a lot in any corporate environment. The words you choose to use speak volumes.

An Exercise to Get You Started

There is an exercise that works very well for getting to the heart of this value business. You can do this alone to determine your personal, added value to the business, and you can do the same exercise with your design staff to come up with ways in which design as a function adds value to any enterprise. The technique is identical either way.

Make a list of every reason you can think of that either you—or the graphic design function—add value to a business. Write down every single thing that comes into your mind. Don't worry at this point about elegant wording, or even relevance. If it comes to mind, write it down. More than likely you will create a fairly lengthy list in very short order. That is always gratifying. I have seen people look at the long list they just generated and say, "Wow, look at all the stuff we do so well!" Put this list aside for a while. Maybe a day or two. Then take it out again and work through the list item by item. Ask yourself for each item, "Does this really, really matter to non-design business people? Do they really care?" If the answer is "No!" then draw a line through the item. I have done this exercise hundreds of times with groups. Let me give you some admittedly extreme (to make the point) examples of items that had to come off the list: "I am really an expert with typography," "I am able to keep many details in my head encompassing multiple projects," "I am friendly and easy to work with," "I use white space very effectively." In a way, all good stuff, but completely meaningless to a business.

I wanted you to put everything down that came into your head for this first pass, because when you draw a line through those items that are really irrelevant, you will have a visual record of the kinds of things you are saying every day that most non-design people really don't react well to. (Refer back to Chapter 2 on becoming multilingual.)

Now is when the excitement about how long your original list was evaporates. You are going to end up with a much shorter list than you expected.

Next, try to work the list again. But this time, do not simply jot down everything that comes into your head. Focus on those items that non-designers would perceive as truly added value. Also, pay more attention to the words you are using to describe each item. This step will take considerably more time than the first go-round. But the results should be equally as exciting. The list will be shorter, but the content will be rich with information about just how design brings added value to a business. Think always in business terms—not aesthetic terms. Just what can design *do* for a business?

Some of the rather strong items I have seen on this second list include: "We shorten the sales cycle." "We visually differentiate our company's products or services in a cluttered marketplace." "We create a powerful competitive advantage." "We clarify the company's business strategy through visual means." This is the stuff that will make senior, non-design business managers sit up and take notice. One rather compelling (if also somewhat non-conversational) statement I have used is: "We are accountable for the visual manifestation of the company's overall business strategy, as approved by the board of directors and the shareholders." That doesn't sound like a simple decorative service to me. It sounds more like a statement from a strategic business group—and that's what you want to become.

Once you have discovered just exactly what your added value really is, begin to incorporate these thoughts into everything you do. Some groups, as John Tyson described, actually develop a "design philosophy" from this exercise. Use these powerful strategic business ideas in memos, presentations, meetings, everyday conversation, and design briefs.

You will often have chance meetings with people in the company who don't know you. Inevitably, they will ask what you do. I try this in class, asking students to tell me what designers do. The first word out of their mouths is almost always, "Umm?" This is followed by something like, "I do graphic design work for brochures (or whatever)." Then they stop, not really knowing where to go with the answer to this question.

After doing this exercise, you should have a whole arsenal of things firmly implanted in your mind that will capture the attention of the person asking the question. Down deep, what you want is for them to become aware of the importance of design to the business, and you want them to say, "I had no idea; I thought you guys were just artists. We should talk some more!"

Many human resource professionals describe a technique called the "two-minute drill." These people argue that in an interview situation, the first two minutes are critical to the outcome of the interview. You must be able to communicate, succinctly and in a compelling way, just what it is you have to offer that is unique. By taking the time to determine the real, added value you offer as a design professional, you will also be able to learn to communicate this value in two minutes or less. It will take some practice, but it is an important component to changing the perception of design in the business world.

To be truly valued in the business world, you absolutely must know what your value is (and we are all valuable!), and you must be able to articulate it clearly and simply in business terms at the drop of a hat. If you really aren't very clear on just why you're a valuable asset, no one else will ever get it either.

Before moving any further through the model, do this exercise. It makes a wonderful agenda item for a design staff meeting. Everyone in your group needs to have the same understanding of your added value. And it beats the hell out of dreary staff meetings where all that happens is each designer gives an endless list of status reports!

Recognize the Business Role of Graphic Design

"Recognize the Business Role of Graphic Design" could also be turned around to say, "Recognize the Role of Graphic Design in Business." Either way you say it, every graphic designer or in-house graphic design manager executing graphic design projects for an enterprise must understand how graphic design adds value to that business. Remember, design is a problem-solving discipline. If your graphic design activities are in support of a business of some type, then the problem to be solved through graphic design will be a *business* problem. Just how far, and in what ways, can design contribute to the solving of a business problem? The answer is, "In more ways than most people think!"

I have a very close friend and colleague who told me very bluntly that at the end of the day, graphic design really couldn't do very much in terms of solving real business problems. My friend is a brilliant business strategist, particularly in the finance arena. He insists that graphic design is necessary only as a vehicle, or environment, to contain information about the company's products or services. His view is not only commonly held, but I would say prevalent in the business world. There are a few companies, of course, whose success depends completely on graphic design—for example, greeting card companies and wallpaper companies. These design-oriented businesses tend to have a built-in appreciation and respect for graphic design. But they are the exceptions.

It is the responsibility of the graphic design professional to change this perception. Frankly, we have done a lousy job of it for years. In order to communicate the role of graphic design clearly, as well as its value, we must first understand the role of graphic design in business.

Just what are the business problems your company is facing? Ask yourself, "What is keeping the CEO awake at night? What are the business issues that are most troubling to him or her?" Then ask yourself, "In what ways can effective graphic design play a role in solving this problem?"

A very common scenario is that designers are separated from business strategy, or that graphic designers are *waiting* for someone to tell them what the business strategy is so they can *react* appropriately. Graphic designers, and particularly in-house graphic design managers, have to become proactive rather than reactive. Graphic design can do very little about increased costs of employee salaries and benefits in the manufacturing plants. But graphic design can do something about costs of raw materials, by specifying different materials, such as paper. Graphic design could eliminate some costs in packaging and print materials. Graphic design can play a major role in presenting the company brand in a more effective and positive way to the target audience.

Many in-house graphic design managers are too concerned about managing the aesthetics of graphic design, and not concerned or involved enough with the hard business issues.

Another Worthwhile Exercise

If you still think graphic design is not really an important component of any business, try this exercise. Get ahold of the company's organizational chart. Don't worry about the names of individuals on the chart—focus on the various functions. For each function, list all of the ways that that function uses graphic design, whether you are accountable for the design solution, or not. The rule is you cannot skip any function on the chart. What you will find is that graphic design does play a meaningful role in each and every function of every business. Every function! If that doesn't demonstrate the role of design in any business, I'm not sure what will. You will discover that a company cannot even exist without graphic design.

I have had people argue that there are functions in a business that do not require graphic design. Take warehousing, for example. Well, are there signs in that warehouse? Do the employees wear uniforms? Are there various forms and documents used to track materials coming in and out of the warehouse? Aren't all of those things designed?

How about employee food services? Do they have menus? Is the company brand printed on napkins and trays? I think you get the point. Graphic design plays a role in *every* facet of any business. Businesses could not survive or function without graphic design. Once again, let me make it clear that I am not advocating that every graphic design group actually do all of the design so essential to every business function. What I am advocating is that the corporate graphic design function be recognized as the experts on design, and should therefore be considered the strategic business center, and principal consultant for all graphic design.

Often during my corporate career, I would call the manager of a particular function, introduce myself, and offer to attend one of their future staff meetings to explain how graphic design played a role in their piece of the business. Often, they were not even aware that they required graphic design on a regular basis. They never thought of design in that way. At the staff meeting, I would take perhaps ten or fifteen minutes to point out how graphic design played a part in their work, and then offer to be a consultant, if needed, on issues they had that involved graphic design. I could help food service find a good resource to print the company logo correctly on napkins, for example. I didn't offer to do the work, just to help them do it well, and correctly, through other resources. This practice accomplished several things:

- It helped large numbers of people understand that graphic design played a role in their daily lives.
- It gave my corporate graphic design function wide visibility.
- It established my graphic design function as a center for expertise.
- I was able to learn firsthand what business issues each function was most concerned about.
- I was able to develop allies all over the company—mutually valuable relationships, if you will, that always served the interests and needs of the graphic design function in future projects.

Mutually Valuable Relationships

Creating mutually valuable relationships all across the enterprise not only for the function of graphic design, but also for the person managing the function, is critical to becoming a strategic partner. However, it is probably the most neglected aspect of the graphic design function I encounter on a regular basis! Graphic designers and graphic design managers seem to have a difficult time in reaching out and being proactive in a business.

When graphic design managers wait until there is a perceived "design crisis" to engage a senior, non-design executive in a conversation about graphic design, they are perceived as a "logo cop." Being perceived as the logo cop is very dangerous. It certainly doesn't help in your quest to be an equal, strategic business partner!

If an in-house graphic design manager is proactive, and instigates meetings with senior managers it will be much easier to develop a strategic business partner relationship in a totally non-threatening, non-confrontational way.

The in-house graphic design manager should not go to such an initial meeting with a copy of the corporate graphic design specs, wearing his or her logo cop badge like a dinner plate! Rather, the graphic design manager should approach a non-design manager as a partner who offers to help him or her using visual design elements, and an ally who is willing to *listen* first, then make creative suggestions as to how to assist the manager in meeting his or her business goals. This becomes a truly mutually valuable relationship.

In many companies there are numerous separate business units. I have found that the people who head these various business units usually want to distinguish their particular business with a unique "look." I am sure you have encountered these heads of business units who want their own distinctive logo, or perhaps their own stationery system, and many want their own business unit newsletter. Down deep, they want to outshine the other business units. This most likely violates corporate Master Brand guidelines, and certainly increases your group's workload. It also leads to confrontations about priority of graphic design products. Once again, the core issue here is these folks regard the corporate graphic design group as a support/service center. They often think you exist primarily to support their particular business and not the entire corporation. The most effective way to deal with these situations is to proactively address their needs. Ask to meet with them. Listen to them. Do not say they are the bad guys for wanting all this unique stuff and attention. That will get you nowhere. Rather, offer to take their needs under serious consideration and come back with a plan to help them achieve some uniqueness while still fitting into the corporate Master Brand guidelines. In essence, you are asking to become their partner in finding realistic solutions. This should lead to future meetings. You will need to develop some well thought-out recommendations which need to be based on real business needs of the company as a whole. Try to be as accommodating as you can, but be prepared to negotiate. Always treat them as a valued partner—a mutually valuable relationship. If you make them feel like you are their enemy, you will get absolutely nowhere.

Use the Organization Chart Exercise Again

When I was discussing ways to establish the role of graphic design in business, I suggested a technique of using the organization chart to review every function in the company, and to determine how each function is dependent on graphic design. I then suggested offering to go to staff meetings of each of these functions to explain how your graphic design function could partner with the staff with respect to its specific needs for graphic design. In a real sense, this is also the best way to develop mutually valuable relationships all across the company. As you visit each group, develop relationships with one or more individuals in that group who might become real supporters of graphic design later on.

One of the strongest alliances I was able to leverage in my corporate career was with the law department. It seems that everything we do in design today has a legal perspective. Wouldn't it be better to have a mutually valuable relationship with the law department than to face the dreaded legal review? If you can partner with one or two corporate attorneys, you will be able to seek the advice and counsel of these partners early in the design process. This will allow a much smoother finish to a graphic design projects. Since the attorneys have partnered with you from the onset of a graphic design project, there should be few, if any, legal issues at the end of the project.

Developing strong and healthy relationships is hard work—and it takes time. It requires tact, listening skills, and the ability to show genuine concern for the other party's needs—not just *your* needs. Above all, it means that a design manager who wants to become a strategic business partner, to be respected and trusted, and to become an important corporate asset rather than a "necessary evil," must take the initiative—and the time—to develop these kinds of relationships. Without *mutually* valuable relationships throughout the organization, you will never really be able to become a core, strategic partner. You will remain a humble service provider.

Implementing Efficient Work-With Processes

Please notice how this heading is phrased: "work-with." This is the opposite of "work-for." We are talking about strategic partnerships, not simply providing a service.

I travel a great deal. Often I will arrive in a city that I haven't visited before. I have a business problem. I am at the airport and need to get to a hotel downtown. Since there is rarely anyone at the counter marked "Information," I walk out to the curb to find a long line of taxis. The taxi driver says where do want to go? I mention the name of the hotel, and the taxi takes me where I want to go. I pay the taxi fare. Problem solved?

What I really wanted was to find a transportation consultant in the information booth. I needed to work with someone who was an expert in local transportation. I could describe my business problem in detail. I am at point A, I need to get to point B, and I have time constraints as well as budget constraints.

Hopefully, the transportation consultant could offer me some creative concepts for solving my problem. There was, of course, the taxi, a direct trip but perhaps a bit high-priced. There might be shared shuttle vans, much less expensive but could take longer than a taxi depending upon how many stops the van would need to make before reaching my destination. There might be a light rail system, cheaper still, but the nearest stop to my hotel would be ten blocks away from the hotel. Several concepts each with both pros and cons. Working with each other we would determine the best concept to meet my business needs.

Too many designers are "taxi drivers;" tell me where you want to go and I'll take you there.

Instead of just driving the cab and telling your "customer" that you'll take them wherever they want to go, you must become a transportation consultant and offer advice on the best way to get there given their needs, time, and budget.

Working *with* someone is quite different from working *for* him or her. All too often, designers and design managers really do believe they are service providers rather than strategic business partners. Believe me, if in your head you think you are a service provider, that's exactly what everyone else will think too. But in addition to *thinking* you are a service provider, if you also *behave* like one, then that's all you and the graphic design function will ever be in the corporate environment.

Nearly every graphic design manager I have ever talked with uses the term "client" endlessly. Let's get it right. They are *partners*—not clients (or customers). Throughout my career, I made a very conscious effort never to think about people I worked with as clients, customers, or subordinates. The people who made up my staff were associates. The people we worked with on graphic design projects were partners.

Partnering on a Global Level

Let us assume you work for a global corporation with offices all over the world. Each of these offices, in all of the various countries, will undoubtedly have specialized needs for graphic design. As the corporate manager of graphic design for the company, you will need to devise a plan to find out just what these special needs are for each country. Of course, the ideal would be to visit each country, but in the practical world that probably won't happen very often.

You will need to identify one or more partners in each country. This will become your own global network. Contact all of these partners, usually electronically, on a regular basis. Keep them informed of graphic design activities, plans, and initiatives at corporate headquarters. Actively solicit their inputs, comments, concerns, and needs as these projects evolve. You will find this a very helpful process. It will also serve to streamline your on-going work.

At Digital Equipment Corporation I instituted this kind of advisory global network for graphic design. It enabled me to speak intelligently in meetings at corporate headquarters about the issues and concerns of the various countries. After one or two years, a senior manager at the company endorsed and supported my efforts to conduct a once-a-year, in-person meeting of all the people in our global graphic design network. A detailed report of the findings from this annual meeting was widely distributed to senior executives at corporate headquarters. This report helped establish our credibility as a knowledgeable, strategic graphic design business partner within the company.

Making Change Possible

All of the stuff we have covered in the model so far is what makes this change possible. We have learned to understand and clearly articulate the true value of graphic design to the enterprise in business terms. We have done exercises to fully appreciate and understand the role of design in the business, not as decoration, but rather as the visual manifestation of the core business strategy. We have proactively sought out key stakeholders in the company, on a global basis, and developed mutually supportive, valuable relationships.

Learning to work with people, to be an effective collaborator and colleague, is easy for some people, but can be very difficult for many more. It requires an innate belief in your expertise, knowledge, and added value to a business. Unfortunately, we are never taught these things in design school. We learn how to be expert graphic designers, but not how to be trusted business colleagues. Just look around at the people who do this well. Lawyers, physicians, CEOs, marketing people, engineers, and nearly all other professionals realize they are necessary because of their expertise. Although under strict dictionary definitions they have clients, they don't behave like these people are their masters. They know the partnership they provide can often make the difference between the success and failure of a business or individual. The graphic design profession has to get to the same place. An "art" service will never be truly valued in the business environment. However, people who make a significant and recognizable difference will be valued.

Should In-House Graphic Design Groups Charge a Fee for Design Work?

Whenever this discussion of working *with* people—rather than *for* them—comes up in my workshops, invariably participants raise the issue of in-house groups being required to charge a fee for their graphic design work. Of course, the folks who work for an external agency must charge a fee for their time. This is how their agency makes money. But how about in-house corporate graphic design groups?

Let me focus on the internal corporate graphic design group first. If we agree that the goal is to become a strategic business partner in the corporation, a valued core competency, and a center for excellence, and to be sought out by every function in the business for advice and counsel about graphic design issues, is that really realistic if we charge for that kind of strategic partnership? I don't believe it is. Once we charge for our time, we go back to being a taxi driver, a provider of "service for hire." If our non-design colleagues in the company have to pay us for our assistance, why wouldn't it be all right for them to go outside of the company and pay the fee to an external agency? After all, they probably think they can get what they like more easily from an outside firm that they are paying.

I really had to suffer with this problem with only one of my corporate positions. When I was hired by Digital Equipment Corporation to head up the corporate design unit of the company, I "inherited" about one hundred people in the group (which also included writers) and a chargeback system that had been in place since the company was founded. An hourly rate for each employee in my group had been established by the finance department. They had determined that, in my group (which they called a "cost center"), each employee had to bill back to other groups at least 68 percent of their available time each week. The figures had been determined by factoring in salaries, benefits, overhead for rent (occupancy charges in the headquarters), and all of the other costs associated with operating a design group (supplies, equipment, and so forth). This is more or less exactly how an external agency has to operate. I found myself running a boutique business inside of a larger business.

Each month I had to prepare complicated forecasts of revenue versus expense. I had to meet with two financial analysts to write a report on my "business." This would take several days of my time on a monthly basis. Internal "customers" would constantly remind me they could take their "business" elsewhere if I didn't give them exactly what they wanted in very short time frames. I realized immediately this system had to go away!

If I wanted to run my own agency, I would have done just that. I would have never joined a large corporation to spend about 80 percent of my time running a not-for-profit business. I wanted to make a contribution to the company as a graphic design guru. I did not want to waste my valuable time concentrating on "making my numbers" each month.

My staff was, likewise, intimidated. They were afraid if they didn't bill out enough time each month, they might be laid off. As a result, they accepted all kinds of what was basically minor production work (name badges for meetings, putting the company logo on gift items, etc.) to ensure that they would have enough billable hours each month. They also had to keep cumbersome daily time sheets that I had to review on a weekly basis. The outcome of all this worry and recordkeeping was less available time to develop really effective graphic design solutions which would benefit the strategic goals of the company.

The process had been well established, and I knew that changing it would take some time and be met with a great deal of resistance, particularly from the finance people. However, I was determined to eliminate the system so that my group could get on with the critical work of doing strategic design for the company.

As part of the solution to this problem, I consulted with a number of my design management colleagues in other companies to determine how they had dealt with the problem. I talked with my friend John Tyson about this, since he had faced the same problem when he reset the design function at Northern Telecom. In the same article by Artemis March, she explained John's strategy this way:

EXCERPT FROM "PARADOXICAL LEADERSHIP: A JOURNEY WITH JOHN TYSON" BY ARTEMIS MARCH

Tyson has committed his group to forging and continually renewing a "clear vision of how our product base is likely to change and learning to be the first to identify the power shifts that will reshape [the] customers' definition of value." "Power shift" is a phrase heard frequently at CDG. Most simply, it means creating disjunctive shifts to future value.

Tyson understands that making a power shift is both an external and an internal process. He communicates his vision of it through distinct language and metaphor: "Metaphor is critical. It is a way to reach when other language becomes ineffective." His use of metaphor is aimed at getting people to switch paradigms, and to affect the internal power shifts that make external shifts possible—indeed, probable.

As Tyson explains it, changing the funding structure of CDG was an essential step in this process:

> We could not be going out with our tin cup. The funding must support the concept because the funding process creates the behavior. If you're a support function, then you shouldn't be surprised to find people selling or being in a reactive mode. Design Interpretive had been funded at the bottom—as subcontractors. So I challenged the organization from the standpoint of my accountability. The day we did the big reorganization, it was important that I stand up there and tell them I had attacked the issue of funding, and that we had reset it completely.

Later in the article, Tyson is quoted as follows:

> "But what happens if you are actually in control? What happens if, instead of going out with a tin cup or chasing golden doors, you go to the same meeting and you say, 'No, you don't understand. I'm not here to get money. I'm here to *invest* in your future'?"

Tyson struck the words "client" and "selling" from the CDG vocabulary. Instead, he says, "Thou shalt use the word 'partner.'" Try lining that up with the tin cup! It doesn't. "Partner" lines up with "investment."

The bottom line is that if you are in a situation as an in-house group that must recover its costs by some kind of internal charge-back system, do everything in your power to eliminate that system. You will never be anything other than a service provider to the company as long as that system exists.

The method I used was to essentially follow my model. I created a presentation for senior management review that began with the *value of the graphic design function to the bottom line of the business.* I gave very clear, businesslike examples of exactly what the role of design was in the business. I enumerated the benefits of mutually valuable, strategic relationships across all functions of the company. I described the numerous advantages of partnering with, rather than working for, key operating units. Finally, I had to prepare a detailed financial analysis and profile of how the new system would be accounted for in the financial reports of the corporation. I won. We became a single expense line on the corporate budget. I no longer had to spend an inordinate amount of time trying to figure out how to make money for my department. Rather, I was able to spend my time trying to figure out how to use graphic design solutions to make money for the corporation.

Get Out into the Real World

In all circumstances—but particularly in global business situations—graphic design managers need to make a concerted effort to investigate various audiences, and to learn how to develop effective design solutions to meet those various audiences' needs. I am a great advocate of graphic design managers and individual graphic designers attending such events as national and international sales meetings and trade shows. Even if the theme of these events does not seem to be directly related to graphic design per se, they are opportunities for the corporate graphic design function to learn more about key stakeholder needs and requirements firsthand.

The days of sitting in a design studio and "just doing" design are long over. The graphic design profession must get out into the world and see what is going on. The design profession must actively listen to key internal stakeholders, as well as members of all of the various target audiences, in order to be able to create effective graphic design solutions for these groups. You can't create brilliant graphic design solutions by simply sitting in a cubicle somewhere. And it's very hard to work with, and design for, people you have never met, seen, or spoken to.

Credibility and Trust

Once you completely understand the added value you offer to any enterprise (personally, and as a graphic design function), once you understand and effectively communicate the role of graphic design in business, once you are able to develop mutually valuable relationships (emphasis on "mutually"), and once you develop the skills to work with people, not for them—then, and only then, will you begin to have real credibility as a strategic business partner.

Knowledge leads to understanding. Understanding leads to appreciation and credibility. Credibility leads to trust. First, people have to have some real knowledge and understanding of what added value graphic design can offer. Only then will they begin to appreciate great design. Credibility stems from providing solutions that really work to meet the business objectives of the project. Once you have credibility, trust is inevitable.

Remember, as I have said time and time again, the core reason so many graphic designers complain that they don't have enough time, don't have sufficient budgets, don't get invited into the process early enough, and aren't appreciated or understood, is because they aren't *trusted* as businesspeople in the first place. Don't forget that any enterprise, for-profit or nonprofit, is in existence solely to make money. A nonprofit business wouldn't be around very long unless it made enough money to pay the bills. A for-profit company, likewise, would disappear very quickly if it didn't make money.

In the minds of business people, the purpose of design should first and foremost be to help meet these business objectives. It is up to the graphic design profession to make them understand that this is our goal too. We need to let our business partners know that the purpose of graphic design is far greater than just being "pretty" or "clever."

Non-designers are nearly always the people who ultimately have final approval of design solutions. Think about that for a minute. People who really don't fully understand what they are approving and have no training or expertise in graphic design end up as approvers of design! Why? Because designers are not trusted to make business evaluations. For the most part, most non-designers *will* admit a professional graphic designer knows more about the aesthetics of design than they do. They just don't trust graphic designers to make the final evaluation of whether their design solution meets real business needs. In order for graphic design to become an equal partner, a co-owner of projects, the graphic design profession must first earn credibility and trust from its non-design partners. The model I have developed has already helped a great many design groups achieve this goal of credibility and trust. It certainly worked for me. Give it a try.

CHAPTER 4

Determining the Real Work of the Function

Nearly every in-house corporate graphic design group I have encountered complains they are understaffed to do all of the design work expected from them. For the most part this is absolutely true.

A major reason for this understaffing is that the "powers that be" do not value graphic design in the ways that they should, and that investing real money in graphic design doesn't seem necessary to them. This is especially true when the graphic design group is considered a necessary evil and, primarily, a service function. Just crank out the work!

In Chapter Three, I outlined a number of ways to reposition in-house graphic design from a service function to a respected strategic business partner.

It is really up to the in-house graphic design manager of the group to take a lead on the next steps. A major next step is to determine the real work of the function, and eliminate those non-strategic projects that should never be accepted by the group in the first place.

So let's get started.

Hopefully, your graphic design group has some written history of projects that have passed through the group. Take a look at the last three years or so of this history. Make a list of every project you have handled. Then code each project as strategic (S), production (P), or nonsense (N). You will want to continue the strategic types of projects, handle pure production work in a new way, and eliminate the nonsense projects.

Let's work backwards. There are just many projects a truly strategic graphic design group should never handle themselves. Some of the nonsense stuff I have encountered include: decorating HQ bulletin boards for holiday events, producing invitations for special corporate events, putting company logos on pencils or pens, producing slide shows for in-house presentations at meetings, decorating the reception area, designing letterheads for some corporate executive's personal use, and many more such activities. Why do I call these things nonsense projects? Because a corporate strategic graphic design function has many more meaningful things to do! All the things I just listed cannot be considered strategically important to the success of the company. Sure, having nice slide shows in internal meetings can be considered important—even critical—to some executives, but there are many resources out there that can create these slide shows without taking up valuable time from an in-house strategic graphic design group.

Don't misunderstand; I am not saying you should not respond at all to these requests. What I am saying is the in-house graphic design manager needs to build a list of reliable internal or external resources that will be happy to produce this stuff. Usually this list of qualified vendors is built by partnering with the Procurement Department (a mutually valuable relationship).Then the in-house graphic design manager either farms this work out his- or herself, or refers the requestor, through the Procurement Group, directly to an authorized outside source. Usually, the in-house graphic design manager remains in the loop by approving this external production work. It's just that the overburdened in-house staff is not saddled with the chore of doing the work.

In my work with numerous in-house graphic design groups we have been able to eliminate 40 percent, or more, of projects handled directly by the in-house group. This percentage becomes extremely meaningful when you are understaffed!

One successful technique is to find a few, qualified, Mom and Pop graphic production resources nearby. Estimate the amount of work you will be sending their way over a one year period. (You can get this estimate from the history exercise you just finished.) Offer them a monthly retainer for the estimated work. Budget for these retainers.

The small production houses will jump at the deal, because they are assured of a monthly, fixed amount of income. Then simply portion out the assignments appropriately. It is a very clean, simple way of moving non-strategic graphic production work out of your department.

Working backwards again, there is certainly a great deal of production work related to your higher level strategic projects which will need to be done by an in-house group.

The most successful system I have seen recently is when the in-house design group re-organizes into three units. There is a strategic design unit, a production unit, and an administrative unit.

High level projects begin in the strategic unit. An experienced strategic designer is assigned a project. That strategic designer will lead the project all the way from conception through production and execution. The strategic designer partners with the project requestor to develop a comprehensive design brief, and then personally does all of the conceptual design work. At a certain point, the strategic designer will need the assistance of a production designer. A production designer from the production unit is assigned to the strategic designer to complete the project. Once this happens, much of the legwork is now being handled by the production designer, freeing up the strategic designer to move on to another strategic project.

A person from the administrative unit is also assigned to the project and handles all of the purely administrative details (project tracking, estimating costs, writing progress reports to stakeholders, print production activities, etc.).

If a project is really not strategic, but needs to be kept in-house, the strategic designer is not needed and the production unit handles the project directly. Examples of this might be updating of price lists, quick updates to an existing piece, producing in-house documents which contain a great deal of confidential and proprietary information, and so forth.

Where I have seen this structure implemented, it has worked very well to help an understaffed department. It works because the real work of the department is better organized and controlled. It is a very efficient system.

A couple of decades or more ago, the project manager, or account manager system, was common in corporate graphic design groups.

The theory was that these project managers or account managers would handle many details, so that fewer trained graphic designers would be necessary. It worked well for quite some time, but the graphic design profession has changed dramatically in the last twenty or more years. Graphic designers today are better trained in strategic graphic design thinking, and overall project management, and are better able to deal directly with the commissioners of a graphic design project. Having fewer production managers or account managers (if you have them at all) might free up head count to hire more graphic designers—both strategic and production designers. I am not suggesting you terminate all of your project/account managers. Rather, as they transition out by retirement or moving on to other jobs, take a careful look at whether it makes sense to replace them, or hire additional strategic or production graphic designers.

Making a Proposal to Hire More In-House Staff

While re-organizing your group, and making arrangements to send small graphic production jobs outside the company, you may need to also seize the day and make your pitch to senior management for hiring a few more in-house designers for your group.

Keep a few things in mind.

You must first firmly communicate—in a compelling way—why graphic design adds value to the enterprise. If management doesn't recognize the business benefit, your request for more staff won't get very far!

Use your new mutually valuable relationships in the company to champion your request.

Make it a sound *business* proposition. Do not say, "It would be better for us if we had more graphic design staff." They won't care what might be better for you. Rather, present a case that demonstrates added value to the *company.* Quicker response to critical shifts in the marketplace, and more visually compelling graphic design solutions to make the customer(s) take notice and want to buy your company's products, are just two examples.

Senior decision makers will be more likely to listen to your pitch if added value to your company as a whole is the top reason for requesting a larger staff. Include as much verifiable financial data you can find to support your request. Be sure to note you have been re-organizing to make your department more efficient. Give sound, business reasons for the need for (and the expense of) a few more graphic design staff.

If you can, benchmark a few other companies of similar size to yours. Determine the volume of these company's graphic design projects, and the number of staff they need to handle the real workload efficiently.

If you can afford it, many in-house groups have engaged an outside consultant to help them formulate a plan to show the need for more staff. For some reason, most corporations often listen more closely to an outside expert then to listen to their own people.

Go back a chapter and re-read the excerpts of the article about John Tyson. John made all the right moves and comments when he reset his design group.

I have a good friend who designs space for corporations. He is very successful! When a corporation engages him to re-design office space for them, he begins by analyzing what each function does; how many present and future staff will be occupying a space; what kind, type, and size of equipment each function requires; and so forth.

What sets my friend apart, and wins him more contracts, is that he is very careful never to quote *cost-per-square-foot* data. Rather, he presents his estimates of *revenue* generated per square foot of space. Folks respond very positively to this approach. He makes a sound business case for increasing revenue. So, stress the potential revenue enhancement, not the increased cost of staff.

Repositioning an in-house corporate graphic design function is not an easy task. There will be a lot of old baggage associated with the "Not the way we have always done it here," syndrome. Change is very difficult for nearly all of us. There is often real comfort in leaving things as they are. But the world does change, and business has changed. The role of graphic design has changed dramatically, and continues to do so. It is up to the in-house graphic design managers and graphic designers to communicate these changes effectively to non-design managers.

Hopefully, you stay up to date with changes in the design world through the Internet and professional design organizations such as the Design Management Institute (DMI), AIGA, and numerous groups on

LinkedIn. As information is published, select pertinent articles and pass them on to the non-design managers. Consider publishing your own, easy to read, internal newsletter, either on-line or in hard copy periodically. Stress, always, enhanced business results due, at least in part, to highly effective graphic design solutions in the marketplace. Or, use the company's internal communications vehicles to highlight graphic design industry activities that have brought greater success, competitive advantage, and improved bottom lines to corporations.

Make "change" a positive for your company. Make "change" a positive for your graphic design group. Remember, it never hurts to have some of your mutually valuable resources inside the company champion your efforts. Enlist their aid and support.

CHAPTER 5

Maintaining the Momentum

LET'S BE POSITIVE! YOU HAVE successfully repositioned your in-house graphic design group from a drop-in service center to a strategic business partner in the corporation. Is that the end of the story? Absolutely not! It is barely the beginning.

This whole re-setting process of your in-house graphic design group is going to take a long time. It will require continual attention to all areas described in my model. You must not expect people to suddenly accept everything about your new positioning. If your group has been regarded as a "service center" for years, perhaps decades, expect skepticism.

There will probably be some of your non-design colleagues who will feel threatened. You have traditionally been a service provider only, and now you are touting your strategic thinking! What does that mean to all those folks who have been used to dropping in with assignments for you? Are they going to lose control of graphic design? Are you trying to invade their turf? Be prepared, lots of people are not going to readily "buy-in" to your new positioning at first. But do not despair. If you keep working diligently, your new strategic partner approach will work.

One of the things I have observed after several years of helping in-house graphic design groups re-structure themselves is that usually it starts off very slowly. In most cases, unless you have the explicit support of very senior management, many folks will just ignore your new ways.

One way to counter this is to enlist the cooperation of just one group in the company that regularly requests design work from your group. Explain all of the benefits that will accrue *to them* by entering into a strategic partnership relationship as opposed to the former service provider relationship. Convince them to participate with you on just one project. It should be a strategic design project. Then do everything in your power to make this new type of relationship work. You will need to be extra careful there are no major "glitches." Your partner needs to feel empowered, not beaten down. Make this one of the most successful projects you have ever undertaken. Then, let your business partner spread the word as to how well everything went, and what a great design solution came out of the process. Hopefully, this will make other design requestor groups willing to give it a try.

Another facet of all this is never simply wait to be asked to execute a graphic design project. You, the in-house graphic design manager, should be on the lookout constantly for ways in which graphic design can impact a business problem your partners are experiencing. Then, be pro-active in approaching them with a proposal of how you can help them.

Just one example might be: a particular product line's sales have dropped off, and their two largest competitors are gaining market share. It is a well-known fact and this information is relatively easy to come by (read industry reports)!

Do a visual audit (visual, because that is your expertise in this problem to be solved) of the competitor's selling materials, advertising, and promotional aids. Compare the competitor's materials to your company's. Determine design strengths and weaknesses for each of the competitors, vis-à-vis the strengths and weaknesses of the graphic design of your company's materials. Then produce a set of *graphic design* recommendations which will make your company's materials stand out from the competitors. Once you have these recommendations, pro-actively take them to the product line manager(s) in your company. Make a highly professional presentation. Only include the graphic design elements. Do not criticize the product line's pricing, advertising campaign, marketing strategy, etc. Keep your presentation focused on what in-house, corporate strategic *graphic design* can bring to an overall solution to the product line's business dilemma.

I have seen in-house strategic graphic design groups do all of this, and then lose the day by infringing on non-design elements which are rightly the sole responsibility of the product line. In short, don't say, "Your crummy product is way overpriced!"

Your role in this strategic partnership is *graphic design*. Keep to your turf, and don't try to take over your partner's turf. If you do, you will lose a partner, and gain an enemy.

By being very pro-active, you will slowly remove the service center mentality you have suffered with for years. Will this pro-activity take a lot of your time? You bet it will! However, if the in-house graphic design manager cannot invest this time, repositioning the graphic design group will never happen. An in-house graphic design manager is just that—a manager. If in your role of graphic design manager you are also executing graphic design projects yourself, you are in for some trouble. Although many of the great in-house graphic design managers I have known are, indeed, wonderful graphic designers themselves, once you reach the point of managing an in-house graphic design group you will not have time to be a hands-on graphic designer too.

Another point is to never say, "No, it can't be done." It is your job to be positive, not negative. It is much better to say, "Here is what we can do," rather than, "We can't do that."

Here is one example of what I am talking about. It is absolutely true, and it happened to me.

Early in my career as an in-house graphic design manger, the United States Government banned a certain ingredient found in common aerosols. As it tuned out, my employer did not use that particular ingredient in our aerosols. However, the government release was very technical and the impression consumers took away was that *all* aerosols were dangerous. The folks who were brand managers for our aerosols—well—freaked out. They came to me and said, "We need a four-color, eight page brochure in huge quantities at every sales office Monday morning next week. This brochure must explain completely why our products are completely safe and exempt from the government ruling." This occurred on the Wednesday morning before the Monday they wanted it delivered all over the United States. It hadn't even been written yet! I made a huge mistake (one of many I made in my early career) and said, "It can't be done by Monday." I think I almost got fired.

One of my mentors said to me, "Peter, you can *never* tell the company it can't be done. Instead, you have to tell them what *can* be done."

I went back to the brand managers and said we can have a black and white piece, one sheet printed both sides that clearly states our products absolutely do not contain the banned chemicals, more information to come soon. Three weeks later we will follow up with a full-color brochure explaining this whole aerosol concern in layman's terms. They bought it! We got the one sheet out by Monday, and completed a very compelling color piece a few weeks later. (Just a side note: we actually won an award for the combined black-and-white piece and color brochure!)

Thanks to my mentor, I learned to never say, "No, it can't be done," again.

Do reposition your group as a strategic partner group. Do enlist support for this effort at the highest level possible in the company. Do expect resistance. Do keep working at making your group believably strategic. Do become highly pro-active. Do expect this will all be a great deal more work for the design manager. Do not give up!

CHAPTER 6

The Collaborative Design Brief

In your efforts to move your department from "drop-in service center" to strategic business partner, you will need to make numerous changes to your former behaviors. One of these is to truly become collaborative—a business partner. A major step in this direction is to revise your thinking about design briefs for strategic projects.

Most likely, when you were in service center mode, requestors of graphic design services would hand you some kind of document which they would call a "brief" for what they wanted. More often than not these briefs were of very little use to you.

I feel so strongly about the collaborative design brief process that I have written a book on the subject, *Creating the Perfect Design Brief*, second edition. This book will give you far more detail than what I will give you here. The subject is so important that I wanted to include some excerpts from the former book in this book.

Once a valid business need that requires design expertise has been identified, and the graphic design group that will execute the project has been determined, the process of creating a design brief must begin immediately.

The very first step is to identify who will assume "ownership" of the project. Ownership means ultimate accountability. If the project is a success, who will accept the praise? If the project fails, who is accountable for the failure?

It is my strong belief that this must be *co-ownership*. There must be an owner who represents the group with the business need for the design work, and a co-owner from the design function that will meet that need. They also must be *equal* partners in the project. It is a strategic business partnership, not a customer service-provider relationship.

Graphic designers and in-house graphic design managers must change their mindset from being service providers, or "taxi drivers," to a mindset of being a strategic, equal business partner. If things go wrong, graphic designers need to stand up and accept accountability.

Client or Partner?

Most graphic designers and in-house graphic design managers I know use the terms "client" or "customer" excessively. "My client wants a light blue background." "My client is very difficult to work with." "My customers never get me involved early enough." "My client doesn't understand design." Using this term tends to telegraph how we are approaching a project. In effect, we are saying we are not in charge of graphic design. "They" are. Why not become equal partners? Why not share the responsibilities—and the accountability?

In my own consulting practice, I make a very sincere effort not to use the word "client." Rather, I talk about "partnering" with people on a project. By strict definitions, of course, these people *are* my clients. I just don't want to think of them that way, and I don't want them to think of me as just a service provider. I want to be their partner.

As is the case with most people, I have a personal physician. One could argue that I am his client. I have medical needs; I pay him a fee for a service to meet these needs. I should be in charge, right? Wrong! If anything, my doctor seems to be far more in charge than I am. Why? Because my doctor has incredible expertise that I don't have. I am the world's greatest authority on how I feel, and my other symptoms. But my doctor is the world's greatest authority on how to solve the problem. Not me. Therefore, we are equal partners. We are both accountable for the outcome of treatment. If I haven't described my problems clearly enough or if I have withheld critical information, the doctor cannot develop the best treatment for me.

It must be the same for the graphic design profession. We must become equal partners—equally accountable—with those people who come to us for our particular expertise, our so-called customers or clients. When we become comfortable with this change in mindset, wonderful, creative things can happen. Great graphic design can happen. Working relationships can become a source of empowerment.

Co-Ownership

It makes no sense to me for someone with a genuine business need for graphic design to write a design brief and hand it to me for execution. It also makes no sense for me to write a design brief without considering the wealth of important knowledge my partner has. Therefore, many years ago, I determined there must be a minimum of two people involved in developing a design brief: someone representing the business needs side, and someone representing the graphic design function.

There are, of course, times when there will be more than two equal partners in claiming ownership of the design brief. There could be a third. This often occurs in situations where there is a business alliance of some type. For example, two airlines form an alliance. Each retains its own brand and identity, but they jointly market some of their products. The marketing materials, which need to be designed to address these shared products, would probably require three equal partners in developing the design brief. In this example that would mean a representative of each of the two airlines and a co-owner representing the graphic design group. But for the most part two people will be all that is required as owners of the design brief.

Although I strongly advocate this co-ownership of responsibility in developing a design brief, I am not advocating design brief development by a large committee, or worse, design by committee. Once a committee feels it is accountable for the actual development and writing of the brief, and for "playing the role of designer," chaos will rule. There will be a number of people on the design brief team, but only two—possibly three—should be owners. The design brief team's responsibility is to give *input* and *approve* the design brief, not to actually write it.

What Level Should the Co-Owners Be?

The level of the individuals appointed co-owners of a design brief might vary depending upon the scope and importance of the project to the enterprise. A senior executive and the manager (or director) of graphic design would most likely manage an annual report to shareholders, or the design of a new, breakthrough product or service. On the other hand, a modification to an existing brochure, catalog, or package might utilize a mid-level marketing specialist and a strategic graphic designer as co-owners. The level of management is not really an issue. The collaborative process of developing the design brief remains the same.

Finally, there is this issue of account managers, or project managers. Many agencies employ people to be account managers—what we used to call the "suits." Should they be co-owners? I have no problem with an account manager being a co-owner of the design brief process, providing the account manager thoroughly understands graphic design, the strategic design process, and the information a graphic designer really needs. Over time, I have encountered account managers who are superb salespeople and very good process managers. Unfortunately, they didn't know much about strategic graphic design thinking. In my opinion, by putting such people between the strategic graphic designer and the business partner, a buffer is formed that is counterproductive to the actual realization of a great graphic design solution. The designer *must* have direct contact with the person(s) he or she is developing a design solution for.

Getting Started

The first step for the co-owners is to meet one-on-one to determine the answers to several key questions. The most important goal of this meeting is to be sure both parties have a very clear understanding of just what this project is all about. Typical questions would include: What are the prime objectives of this project? Why is this project necessary? Why is it necessary to do this project now? What *business* outcomes do we want? What are the most critical aspects of this project? Finally—and this is very important—who are all of the stakeholders in this project? For the most part, this type of information is either not included or is very vague in a Request for Proposal (RFP). This is yet another reason for not considering an RFP—and the resulting proposal—an adequate design brief.

RFPs Versus Design Briefs

It is not uncommon for a corporation to issue a Request for Proposal (RFP) for graphic design work. Often these RFPs are sent to more than one external graphic design agency, and also to an in-house group as well. An RFP outlines, too often in very general terms, a brief description of the project, the budget, the time frame, and exactly what the company is looking for in the design solution. Then, each recipient of the RFP is asked to submit a written proposal as to how they would meet the parameters of the RFP. Based upon a review of the proposals submitted, the company awards a contract for the project to one of the respondents. This is all fine and good for many situations, but these proposals are definitely not design briefs. Once a contract has been awarded, the winner will still need to meet with the company representative and develop a proper collaborative and complete design brief. This brief will include much of what was in the RFP and resulting proposal, plus a great deal more. It is still a partnership.

What Must Be in a Proper Design Brief?

It makes no sense to me to be a co-owner of, and therefore accountable for, a project without knowing the answers to many questions. Yet, as I have been involved with graphic design projects for all kinds of businesses over the years, it is startling how many times the answers to these questions are not clear at all. Let's take a closer look at each of these core questions.

What Are the Prime Objectives of the Project?

In nearly every case, there is some sort of working title for the project, such as "Design a new brochure for xyz product," or "Create a series of sales sheets for a new product." With all the renewed interest in brands and branding, a common request get is, "Can you design a logo for me?" That's all well and good. It's nice to know, in broad terms, what we are doing. Why do you need a logo? What are you trying to accomplish with this new logo? What are the *prime* objectives for this project? What was keeping someone awake at night that generated the need to initiate this graphic design project?

For example, if the company is asking for a new brochure is it simply because we just routinely do a new brochure every six months? Or does the current brochure contain outdated information that must be revised? Perhaps the current brochure has been ineffective in the marketplace. Why? Is the product or service new and has no brochure yet? What is this new logo supposed to convey visually? How will this logo relate to corporate branding? As a designer, I need to know *why* we are being asked to do this project. If I don't understand why I am doing something, I probably won't do a very good job. If design is a problem-solving discipline, then I need to know exactly what the problem is. In my career, primarily in print projects, I have been amazed at how many of my partners had to admit they really didn't know what the prime objectives were either. I would get vague responses such as, "The VP of marketing told us to create a new brochure." Or, "Sales reports the current brochure hasn't been very successful." Okay, yeah—exactly why does the VP believe we need a new brochure? Or, just what do the salespeople find is not working in the current edition?

One of the many advantages to this collaborative design brief process is that these questions can be asked in a non-confrontational, non-threatening environment. After all, nothing has been done yet! We are simply in the very preliminary stages of developing a design brief. On the other hand, if I wait until we are halfway through a project to ask what the prime objectives are, I will look pretty foolish. It's totally reasonable to begin with these simple questions, and to come to an agreement about the answers. If the objectives aren't clear at this preliminary meeting, it should be clear to the co-owners that the answers must be found before we go too much further.

Why Is This Project Necessary, and Why Is It Necessary Right Now?

These questions may sound deceptively simple and unnecessary, but they really are not. Timing will become a major aspect of the design brief we are about to create, and I, for one, want a good grip on the urgency associated with the project. If the urgency is genuinely great and therefore the time frame very short, this will dramatically affect the amount of time I can spend on design concept exploration and development. I need to know this *now*.

Unfortunately, a great many graphic design projects are assigned rather arbitrary deadlines. Some senior executive has said, "I want this in two weeks." If there isn't some earthshaking reason for this arbitrary due date, I want my partner and I to negotiate a realistic time frame to complete this project. How many times have you rushed to meet some deadline, only to discover there is now new information, or someone "doesn't like the design," and suddenly there is another two or three weeks available to make changes!

It is very critical to learn to negotiate realistic due dates.

What Business Outcomes Are Expected from This Project?

Note that we are talking about business outcomes, not aesthetic outcomes. We are *not* doing design exploration in this meeting. Typical business outcomes may include objectives like: shorten the sales cycle, enhance competitive advantage, increase market share, firmly establish a leadership position, and so forth. Whatever the business reason for the project given, the key question from the graphic design co-owner should be, "How?" How will this project shorten the sales cycle? How will it enhance competitive advantage? How will it increase market share? Your partner, representing the business side of this equation, must have some thoughts on these subjects, and you need to be certain that you are both on the same page with realistic expectations. There are times when people expect miracles from graphic design that are just not going to happen. Graphic design can certainly contribute to meeting these business objectives as long as you have told me what the objectives are, but graphic design alone may not be able to do it all!

I have actually had marketing people say to me (too many times), "We think that if we had a really snazzy, colorful, brochure that will knock people's socks off, we'll blow the competition out of the water." What does that mean? Tell me what you think "snazzy" is, and why that will make a difference. I'd also like to know why you think a snazzy brochure would give you some kind of business advantage. What quantifiable data is available to substantiate your personal opinions?

What *exactly* is the problem to be solved?

Identify Key Stakeholders

Finally, in this initial meeting, my partner and I need to identify all of the key stakeholders in this project. The list is often longer than you would think. Identifying these people up-front will allow you to develop some key strategies, which I discuss in more detail in my design brief book. But it will also give you the opportunity to build these stakeholders into the phase process of the project at the most appropriate time. Permit me to give you some examples to think about.

Nearly all design projects today involve lawyers. There are copyright issues, intellectual property rights, trademarks, patents, and so forth. Will you utilize stock photography? If so, what kind of rights do you want for the images? Will you use external vendors or suppliers? Will there be contracts? Will a legal review be necessary prior to approval of the final graphic design solution? It's kind of difficult not to involve lawyers in business graphic design projects these days. They are stakeholders. At what point will they need to be involved? How much time will they need to do their work? Is part of the overall project budget allocated to these key stakeholders for their activities? If so, how much has been allocated? Will they consult with you on an ongoing basis, or just show up at the end to tell you to make changes?

Other stakeholders include people like the sales organization, manufacturing, procurement (we used to call it "purchasing"), distribution channels, and approvers. The list will be much longer. But you don't want to find out at the last minute that warehousing and distribution have a three-month lead time to accept print materials into their systems! All stakeholders need to be identified up-front, then asked right away to provide detailed information about their issues, concerns, constraints, and needs.

Some Essential Elements to Include in the Design Brief

In addition to the questions listed above, every design brief should include:

- An executive summary and overview of the project and the background information that led to the decision to do this project
- A brief review of current industry or category developments
- A thorough discussion of the target audience(s). Exactly who are they? A woman eighteen to twenty-five years old is not sufficient!
- What other existing materials in the company portfolio will be used with this new piece?
- A list of quantifiable business objectives, coupled with a design strategy, to meet each of these business objectives
- Project scope, time line and budget (phases of the project)
- Any pertinent research data pertaining to this particular project
- Details about direct competitors similar offerings

There may be many other things that need to be included in a good design brief. These will vary by specific project. The important thing to remember is that a graphic designer needs to know everything possible about the project prior to beginning any graphic design work.

It's Like Stir-Fry Cooking

I have a colleague who compares a good design brief to stir-fry cooking. The stir-fry technique of cooking is very fast. (Sound like any projects you have had to do?) My colleague tells us that before you can begin to stir-fry cook a meal, you must first assemble *all* of the ingredients. You cannot heat up oil in a wok, add a few ingredients, and then realize you forgot the chicken! The meal will be ruined, and you will have to go out and buy some chicken, and then start all over again.

The collaborative design brief process is designed to make sure that you and your business partner have *every* ingredient necessary for the graphic design project before you begin cooking. If you have everything you need for the graphic design project up front, the actual design work can proceed more quickly.

Design Is Only One Ingredient of a Successful Business

Years ago, when I managed the graphic design function at the Gillette Company, I had a mentor. We created sales collateral material, retail point-of-purchase (POP), and display materials, and worked on some packaging projects. My mentor told me that the graphic design projects we were doing were actually just ingredients in the selling process. In order for all of the business objectives to be met, a combination of key ingredients would be necessary, but they all had to work together seamlessly. Of course, he was right. I had designers in my studio who really believed a product sold well only because of the package, brochure, or in-store display. It's always more than that. But for graphic design to do its part effectively, the graphic design function has to completely understand all of the other ingredients. Designers must learn to ask questions about all of these other key ingredients. What does the advertising look like, and what are the key messages in the ad? What kind of PR will be used in the sales cycle? What marketing or sales techniques will be employed? Precisely how will graphic design support and work with all of these other activities?

One of the things my mentor asked me to do was spend a few days each year traveling around with salespeople to observe actual sales calls. I also visited retail stores to talk with store managers about how they used POP and display materials. This became an absolute priority for me over the years. How could I design or manage design for sales collateral materials if I had never been on a sales call with a salesperson from my company? As a graphic designer, I need to thoroughly understand that whole experience. I also sent my design staff on similar expeditions into the land of the target audience. It made a huge, positive difference in our graphic design solutions. If I wanted to be considered a core, strategic business partner, and I wanted graphic design to be perceived the same way, then I needed to become an expert in the whole business process. Not just a "taxi" driver. Not just a service provider. Not just a clever artist.

Partners Need to Understand Each Other

The question about what the critical aspects of the project are in the mind of my co-owner is also important. If my partner believes the brochure must be very colorful, I want to know why he or she believes this is true. I want to know now, before we start the design process. If I agree with his or her rationale—all well and good. However, if I believe the door must remain open for other concepts, then I want to be able to negotiate for this creative freedom now. Doing it now will save a lot of time, frustration, and hard feelings later. By the same token, it is incumbent on me to help my partner understand the graphic design/creative process. The partner relationship must be completely open and candid. Remember, understanding leads to appreciation!

The Design Brief Project Team

Now that the co-owners/partners have had their preliminary meeting, it is time to determine who will be part of the design brief project team. The stakeholder list will be useful to do this. Obviously, you won't be able to include everyone on your stakeholder list as a project team member. But you should be able to identify ten or twelve key stakeholders who really must be involved from the beginning. There will also be designers, writers (perhaps), and production support people who will actually be involved in the day-to-day execution of the project. This design brief project team needs to be kept relatively small or you will never get anything done. So choose the team with great care. Be sure that the most important stakeholders are included.

Participants in my seminar on this topic often comment that they would never have the time to engage in this type of meeting. My answer, once again, is that you *have* to take the time. Whatever time you spend on this preliminary meeting will be returned to you tenfold later on. This first design brief project team meeting should only require a couple of hours of your time. Once you have established a mutually valuable working relationship with your partners, future design brief project meetings should be very brief.

After you are used to working this way, you will be amazed by how quickly you can get started and how truly efficient this process can be. What is the average investment of time to develop a collaborative design brief? Usually about four to six hours. However, remember this process will eliminate a lot of confusion and misunderstandings later on. This up-front time investment should save you many times the time investment later on.

The next step is to assemble your design brief project team. In the ideal world, this would be a roughly two hour meeting with all the team members present in the same room. Email and other forms of technology have their places, but there is nothing like a good face-to-face discussion to get things moving quickly! I suggest two team meetings be scheduled. At the first meeting, a number of questions will undoubtedly come up that need a little time to answer. This will require a second meeting to discuss the answers to those questions. After this second design brief project team meeting, team members will stay informed through technology such as email and telephone conference calls. Actually, unless there is an emergency, you may not need to assemble the whole team in one room again.

The agenda for the design brief project team meeting is fairly simple. The co-owners introduce themselves and the other team members (unless they all already know each other). Next, the co-owners review the details of the project that they discussed in their preliminary meeting. Review what we are doing, why we are doing it, what the business objectives and outcomes are, and who the stake-holders are; then identify who will actually be doing the design work. Mentioning just who will be *accountable* for certain activities is also critical. Everybody in the room can't be accountable for everything in the project!

At this point, the design brief project team is invited to comment and/or ask questions. Each member of the team should also be asked for his or her specific inputs to this project. A word of caution here. This is not a meeting to design anything. It is merely a meeting to develop scope and timing, and to solicit business input. There will be questions with no apparent immediate answers. More than one person will say, "I'll have to get back to you on that." That's fine. Once again, that's why we are going to have a second meeting. The key is to be sure someone has been identified to get the answers, and a specific date for delivery of those answers has been established.

There are some ancillary benefits to this kind of meeting. First of all, everyone likes to be consulted and to feel a sense of participation in a project. At this stage, no one can really do much harm. We are just informing people something is *about to* happen, and their input and expertise is welcomed. Later on, you won't have to listen to people who say, "If you had only asked me, I would have told you that . . . ." Secondly, non-design stakeholders will begin to perceive the design function as partners, not simply decorative service providers.

Once this first team meeting has been conducted, the co-owners can go off to begin actually drafting the design brief. This first draft will be presented at the second team meeting.

It is important for me to say here: There is no single, off-the-shelf format for a design brief. The actual format that you will develop on your own will vary depending upon your company's standards, practices, and culture, as well as the type of graphic design project itself. Some organizations prefer a brief that is narrative in nature. Others prefer bulleted lists. Many incorporate graphs, charts, or illustrations. Others do not. However, the key ingredients for the content of a perfect design brief are the same no matter how you format the final document.

It's also important to note that there will be times, depending on the nature of the project and the graphic design group involved, when some of these key ingredients will not be included. There may also be some ingredients not mentioned here which you shall decide should be included. At the end of the day, each organization needs to develop its own format and list of ingredients.

As mentioned, the co-owners actually create the first draft of the design brief and determine the design brief format that will be used. If the whole design brief project team tries to sit down and write the first draft as a committee, you will never get the brief finished.

Following the first design brief project team meeting, the co-owners create the first draft of the brief in the particular format they have chosen, recognizing that there will undoubtedly be some missing information. The first draft will be reviewed with the whole design brief project team at the second previously scheduled team meeting. This will allow team members to add their inputs and supply missing information. The goal is to have a final, unanimously agreed upon design brief at the end of the second meeting. This process will also ensure that all critical information is indeed supplied for the design brief and that the information is current, accurate, and truly useful to everyone involved.

Of course, changes and additions might have to be made to the design brief document throughout the course of the project. This is inevitable. But by getting unanimous agreement on the essential content of the design brief prior to starting the design process, these inevitable changes can be kept to a minimum.

Remember, the co-owners are accountable for the whole project. Only the co-owners can approve any changes to the brief.

FAQ

Question: How can a design brief be used to measure the ROI of a design project?
Answer: A well-developed design brief will fully describe the problem to be solved with design, the core business objectives to be realized, and the desired outcomes, or results desired upon implementation of the design solution. It will be these things that will determine the criteria for measurement of the design monetary investment in the design.

Question: How do I determine if a design brief is really needed for a new project?
Answer: If a design project's scope is very limited, perhaps just a minor fix or two to an existing product, a design brief will probably not be necessary. However, if the project entails creating an entirely new design solution, a design brief will be critical.

Question: Why is it so important for a design brief to be co-developed by both the commissioner of the design project and the designer?
Answer: Each party brings specialized knowledge and skill sets to the project. By collaborating on the development of a brief, a great deal of time is saved during the execution phase since nearly all questions have already been raised and dealt with efficiently by both parties.

Question: We never have time to engage in a lengthy brief development process. Are their any short-cuts?
Answer: Actually, no. If the project is critical enough to commission in the first place, embarking on a collaborative brief development process is paramount to the eventual success of the effort. The time saved in the execution of a design project will be far greater than the time spent developing a great brief first.

Question: Why do we need to test design concepts with the target audience?
Answer: People who are part of the company developing the design are too close to the project to make a truly objective decision of which design concept will work best. Only the people you are designing for, your target audience(s), can really let you know if your concepts will work for them.

Summary: Ten Basic Rules for the Design Brief Process

My very basic tem principals of developing the perfect design brief include:

1. It is essential that the development of the design brief be a collaboration between the two accountable parties in the project. One owner represents the *business need* for commissioning the design project in the first place and the other person must represent the design function that will actually create the final design solution.

2. The completed brief must include all of the essential ingredients to *inspire* a core creative concept. The brief leads to the inspiration for this concept development.

3. The brief must be a strategic, business document. It must clearly define the overall business objects which led to the need for commissioning the project.

4. Target audiences are the most often misrepresented elements of the brief. Just who will be using, or reacting to the design solution? Cursory descriptions such as women eighteen to

twenty-five, executives, or homeowners, are hardly sufficient! A comprehensive section on the target audiences is critical, but often all but ignored.

5. A listing of the specific business objectives for the design project should be married to design strategies to meet each business objective, and then criteria for measuring success added for each entry.

6. It must be kept in mind that design actually does follow a logical process. By breaking this process down into defined phases, and including time and cost allocated for each phase, reasonable and realistic time frames and budgets can be developed for the entire process. The phases also provide a good place to insert target audience testing of concepts along the way, and to permit various stakeholders to be involved in progressive approvals.

7. A really good design brief should be as long as it needs to be to be useful. Many companies specify a brief should not be more than two pages. Two pages will never be enough!

8. The brief should contain detailed information on the competition. What are the competition showing and saying? Why would your audience prefer your solution to your competitors? This generally means that an early phase must be a competitive audit.

9. There are many levels of complexity for a design brief. Some projects will require a rather extensive brief. Others may require less time to develop. There is no "one size fits all" in considering design briefs.

10. Involve all stakeholders in the design project before developing the brief. Their up front input can help you avoid costly delays during the actual design process.

CHAPTER 7

An Example of a Design Brief

At every presentation of my seminar on design briefs, invariably one or more people ask if I can show them a "perfect" design brief. The simple answer is, "No, I cannot." There are several reasons for this. First of all, there is no such thing as a single example of a "perfect design brief." A design brief becomes *perfect* only when you have constructed it very carefully with your co-owner/partner and it has performed well for you for a *specific* project. *Then*, you might call it perfect.

The next most important reason I can't show a perfect, real example is that no company in its right mind would let me publish such a brief in a book or distribute copies at a seminar. As you now know, a really good design brief contains a great deal of proprietary information about a company's business strategy, results of research data, and future plans. This is not the kind of information companies are willing to share. Design briefs are highly confidential documents. Although I have personally seen a great many good design briefs, and I certainly have been part of the development of hundreds of them, the companies I have worked with always have me sign confidentiality agreements that prohibit sharing their information outside of that company.

The best I can do is to completely fabricate a fictitious brief for an imaginary company. What follows is just such an imaginary brief. I have used the information for the background and objectives section from a real company that I quoted previously as a starting point. It is a fairly typical design problem for some companies, and the source (the name of the company) is completely transparent. From there, I have fabricated everything else. My only purpose is to demonstrate about how long a brief might be if you only included the basics I covered previously. I have added some annotations (in italics) for each section as a type of review of the critical elements. It would also be best to assume that this would be the first draft presented to the design brief project team for discussion and approval. Such a team might want to add some material, revise the wording, or delete some material, as I described earlier. Once again, think of this only as an example of a *starting point* for a brief.

I have also chosen to use the narrative format, since that is the one I personally favor. Remember, you can develop any format you like, as long as it is clear and works well for you and your company.

Please do not assume that this example is in any way reflective of any particular company or industry category. It is just an example, I have used many times before.

ACME COMPANY

Design Brief
Total Redesign of Company Portfolio

Project Overview and Background

The current company portfolio reflects a series of different visual treatments that were created at various points in time to fulfill various business objectives and strategies. As a result, the portfolio lacks visual cohesiveness and clarity. This exacerbates target audience confusion within the complicated and already cluttered global marketplace for these products. In order to achieve clarity and cohesiveness, and to shorten the sales cycle, increase competitive advantage, improve market share, and thus enhance the bottom line, the entire portfolio must be redesigned at one time, utilizing an umbrella strategy. Design principles and strategy for future new products must also be established within this umbrella strategy.

The ultimate design solution will consistently incorporate company branding elements, achieve a cohesive visual appearance across the line, and clearly distinguish the different products within this umbrella strategy.

In order to most efficiently execute this project, the redesign will be conducted in eight phases:

- Phase 1—Complete visual audit of existing company portfolio as well as a visual audit of the top three competitors' portfolios.
- Phase 2—Develop a maximum of six creative design concepts that meet project business objectives.
- Phase 3—Test all concepts with target audiences.
- Phase 4—Select three concepts and further refine each. Retest all three with target audience.
- Phase 5—Select one concept, fully develop it, and perform final testing.

- Phase 6—Develop approval presentation.
- Phase 7—Implement approved design solution.
- Phase 8—Develop measurement metrics.

The project is scheduled to be completed by (date). The budget for this project has been set at (amount).

Project owners shall be (name), vice president of marketing, and (name), strategic design director.

Design brief project team members will include: (list of names/titles of each team member)

Note: As mentioned before, this section also serves as the executive summary of the project.

Category Review

The ABC category is a $60 billion industry worldwide. Although there are more than 125 brands competing in this category, only four brands are considered market leaders. These four brands collectively account for 65 percent of the total market.

Brand X is the current market leader, with a 25.5 percent share of the market. Brand X was the third company to enter this category when the category was developed forty-seven years ago. Within seven years, Brand X had acquired the first two competitors to enter the market, making Brand X the dominant brand worldwide. Within five years of Brand X's initial acquisitions, more than thirty other companies entered the rapidly growing category. Demand for these new products by consumers more than doubled each year for the first decade. Brand X had achieved dominance primarily because it was one of the original brands in the category; it had the widest distribution system, which ensured their products were available virtually everywhere; and it had very high brand recognition and recall by the target audience.

Brand Y is the second largest competitor, with a 15.5 percent total share of the current market. Brand Y has achieved its current position primarily through very aggressive marketing and promotion techniques. Brand Y utilizes extensive couponing and discounting programs worldwide, making their offerings appear somewhat less expensive than the others.

Brand Z and our company, ACME, are tied for third place, with a market share of 12 percent each. Brand Z is somewhat older than the number two brand, Y. Brand Z has been in the market for twenty-eight years, and Brand Y has been in the market for twenty years. Brand Z has wide distribution, primarily through mass market discount chains worldwide. Brand Z's product line is considered less expensive than the other leading brands. Brand Z competes primarily on price considerations.

ACME Company is sixteen years old. Our company has achieved its number three position largely through aggressive marketing and advertising focusing on superior quality and craftsmanship. ACME has not traditionally offered deep discounting and does not use coupons in the marketplace. ACME products are priced at parity with Brands X and Y.

The balance of the competitors in the marketplace have generally existed less than ten years as a brand, and most of them tend to be more regional than national or global.

Although demand for these products grew rapidly for nearly twenty years, the market is now declining slightly. This is primarily due to a weak economy in most parts of the world, and shifting consumer needs.

Industry business analysts predict that many competitors will gradually drop out of the market over the next five years. Some brands will be acquired by the top three brands, and others will simply cease doing business. Analysts predict that no more than twelve brands will ultimately survive in the marketplace.

It is incumbent on the top four brands, including ACME Company, to ensure their continued presence in the marketplace by strengthening their positions through product improvements and more compelling "reasons to purchase."

Notes: More than likely, the content of this section has come from a market research group or other marketing function within the company. So just why is this category review description helpful to designers?

Primarily because it is a brief summary of what has happened as well as what is happening right now in the category. One of the important points that a designer or design team could take away from this particular example is that the market is quite large—$60 billion. This is particularly significant because it means the category has major visibility in the consumer market place. Obviously people are looking for these products worldwide.

A designer should also recognize that with 125 brands competing, there must be a great deal of visual clutter in this space, and that means the design must be visually prominent, distinctive, and "different" from all of these competitors. However, we learn that there are only four major brands. And we learn that ACME is tied for number three in total market share. This signals that ACME primarily needs to study these four brands very carefully in their visual audit.

It should also be significant to designers that the category is nearly a half-century old. The category leader is forty-seven years old. This means that it has considerable brand equity in its visual appearance and might encounter difficulties if it tried to come up with a "whole new look." ACME also has this problem. ACME is a quarter of a century old, and also enjoys strong visual equity in its brand. Translation: ACME needs to proceed with caution if it tries to stray too far from its established brand identification.

Another critical area to designers in this category review is that the vast majority of competitors are relatively new, and therefore not as well known as the leaders. They would have considerably more freedom than the current category leaders in presenting themselves as highly contemporary, forward-thinking, leading-edge, and even "experimental."

We also learn that the number one brand in the category has traditionally been very aggressive in the marketplace. It has bought out the early market leaders to eliminate that competition. It is constantly promoting with discount offers. This means it is trying to maintain its position by a reduced price strategy. It is also everywhere! Its superior distribution system ensures that no matter what store a consumer goes into, that brand is always available. Therefore, it is easy to find and easy to purchase. ACME has followed a business strategy of not discounting in favor of a message that it is the highest-quality producer, and therefore worth the premium price of the product. As ACME designers begin to develop concepts for redesigning the whole portfolio, this fact will be critical. Their new designs will have to carry through this theme of "superior quality."

Finally, the category has flattened out. It is more than likely that there will not be many new brands entering the market; in fact, many current brands may cease to exist in a few years. ACME Company will most likely survive, so it needs to be sure to consider some classical, more timeless design concepts. While newer companies can explore highly contemporary design treatments, ACME will need to ensure its new design concepts are not trendy or fads of the moment. In 2015, ACME cannot afford to have people saying that ACME looks like a 2003 brand, or that ACME is old-fashioned. On the other hand, ACME does want to make its visual image more contemporary, while still communicating that it is well established and has been around for a very long time.

All of these points, and possibly others, will need to be discussed by the design team prior to exploring concept development. The category is complex. ACME will need to look fresh and up-to-date, but not trendy. The message of superior quality will have to come through loud and clear in all treatments. ACME will need to leverage its heritage, but at the same time update its image. Obviously, all of this creates a major design challenge. The category review is well worth the time it will take to discuss in-depth!

Most likely, your company's market research group or marketing group will provide most of this category review for you. It is then up to the design brief project team, as well as the design team, to analyze the category review for clues that will help them develop initial concepts.

Target Audience Review

ACME Company's product line is considered a basic necessity for the care and maintenance of living quarters. Nearly every apartment, private home, hotel, inn, etc., will have one or more of these devices. For this reason, the target audience does not include young children or individuals living in someone else's home. Generally, the youngest male or female who would purchase or use one of these products is college age (eighteen years plus) and occupying his or her first living space away from home. These younger individuals tend to purchase our lower-priced models, which are very basic devices. As the target audience, consisting of both males and females, sets up more permanent housekeeping, this audience tends to look for either our mid-priced models, or possibly our most expensive models. The average age of consumers in this latter category is twenty-four to thirty years old. As our target audience matures, it will tend to give more consideration to our more expensive models, which have a variety of options available. The average age of individuals who consider this type of upgrade is forty to sixty years. While the primary purchase decision maker was female twenty or more years ago, today both sexes can be considered primary decision makers.

The degree of sophistication and education of those who purchase our product is important. Our superior models, with a wide array of options, tend to be purchased by individuals with college degrees beyond the bachelor's level. The basic models, purchased by all age groups, are more likely to be purchased by individuals who want simplicity of operation, basic performance, and low cost.

Specialized versions of our product line, especially the very small handheld units, have more appeal to individuals who live in motor homes, or for use on boats. These handheld models are also popular with college students who live in dormitory rooms or studio-sized apartments.

Another category of the target audience that must be considered is professionals who are hired to maintain larger living spaces or office buildings. This category prefers the larger, more "industrial strength" models, regardless of initial cost.

Our product line is considered a consumer durable product; therefore, individuals only purchase an average of four units in their lifetime. The market trend is for people to initially purchase a basic, low-cost model, and then upgrade two or three times to the more advanced models. Income levels of the target audience tend to increase in ten-year intervals, beginning at the lower end of age twenty to thirty, advancing each subsequent decade, and leveling off at approximately age sixty. Elderly people (ages seventy plus) often return to the basic models because of their ease of use and low cost.

For all segments of the target audience, consumers are most interested in: ease of use, durability, overall performance, cost, warranty, readily available repair service, and functionality.

The younger consumers (eighteen to thirty) are most interested in sporting events, social events with peers, watching videos, popular music, and domestic travel. Our target audience in the age group between thirty and fifty report that its primary interests include: foreign travel, outdoor events including skiing, aquatic sports, and boating, reading, attending cultural events such as the theater, and home improvement projects. Consumers over the age of fifty tend to spend more time at home (or in a vacation home), watching television, reading, and participating in community activities.

Note: This section also provides a great deal of useful information for the design team. ACME Company has several tiers of its basic product, from low-end models to "industrial strength" and luxury models. The typical ages, income, interests, and level of education and sophistication are described for each tier of the product line. It is always important to remember that this kind of audience description is always based on averages from market research. It can never be absolute. It is meant more as a guideline. For example, there could very well be a young consumer who wants, and can afford, the most luxurious model of the product, even for his dorm room at college.

However, for a project such as this one, it is necessary for the designers to discuss each of the types of audience described as typical for a particular product. For example, how would—or should—package design differ for each group in the target audience? What are the implications from the comment that both males and females buy the product? Does this mean graphic concepts should be gender neutral? Why or why not?

Another interesting point for discussion that could be extracted from this target audience review is that the basic models appeal primarily to very young consumers who are entering the market for the first time, as well as to the very elderly consumer who is no stranger to the market and has used the product for years. What does this mean to a design team? Should the various design elements of the product (the product itself, the packaging, the sales collateral material, etc.) be geared more toward one age group than the other? How can the design become appealing to both groups? How big an issue is this anyway? What are we going to do about it? How should we approach this issue?

These design concept discussions have to come from the material supplied largely by marketing people who did not have design specifically in mind when they did their research. This becomes another added value of a strategic design function—to take largely marketing-driven research and extract design strategy from what is available. As I mentioned in Chapter 3, this is why a short phrase in response to target audience description, such as "women twenty to fifty," isn't useful to a design team. There just isn't any jumping-off place for meaningful, strategic design discussion.

Company Portfolio

The entire ACME Company portfolio consists of 100 discrete stock keeping units (SKUs). This project will not involve the redesign of any product. Rather, the redesign project will focus only on packaging, collateral sales literature, retail in-store display items, catalogs, and owners' manuals. The 100 SKUs include:

- **Basic Line:** one full-size unit, one handheld unit, one commercial full-size unit, and one commercial handheld unit, for a total of four discrete products. These are well-engineered basic units with no frills, accessories, or other options.

  They are the lowest-cost units, with a suggested retail price of $40 for the basic full-size unit, $30 for the basic handheld unit, $65 for the heavy-duty full-size basic commercial unit, and $55 for the commercial handheld unit.

- **Mid-price Line:** one full-size unit, one handheld unit, one commercial full-size unit, and one commercial handheld unit, for a total of four discrete products. In addition, each of these four mid-price units are available with up to five optional attachments, each sold and priced separately. Including the optional attachments, the mid-price line includes a total of twenty-four SKUs. The entire mid-price line has slightly better engineering of components. The optional attachments are not compatible with any product in the basic line.

The mid-price line suggested retail price is $125 for the full-size unit, and $175 for the commercial full-size unit. Handheld versions are priced at $100 and $140 for the commercial unit. The five optional accessories for each of these products are priced from $30 to $80 each, depending upon the functionality of the accessory.

- **Luxury Line:** one full-size unit, one handheld unit, one commercial full-size unit, and one commercial handheld unit, for a total of four discrete products in the luxury line. In addition, each of the standard items in the line are available with up to five optional attachments, each priced separately. The luxury line also includes three color options: white, gray, and blue. The color options are available for both the main unit as well as the optional accessories. The luxury line consists of seventy-two SKUs, including accessory options and color options.

  The luxury line suggested retail price is $430 for the main unit and $550 for the commercial version. The handheld units retail for $375 and $500 for the commercial version. Accessories range in price from $80 to $250, depending on the accessory. There is no additional charge for choice of color. The luxury line features state-of-the-art engineering, highest-quality components, a lifetime warranty for parts and labor for any component that fails due to manufacturing defects, and a standard leather storage bag for both the main product as well as the accessories.

ACME Company utilizes a monolithic brand strategy with all products employing the ACME brand. ACME is not involved with any other type of product. ACME Company is publicly held, and governed by a board of directors elected by shareholders. Stock prices have risen to a high of $93 over the past year. Current stock price for the last quarter is $57.

ACME's primary competitors offer essentially the same range of products and accessories. Brand X, the market leader, does offer limited accessories for its basic line of products. Brand X also heavily promotes its commercial line of products to noncommercial consumers. Brand Y does not offer accessories for its basic line of products; Brand Y often offers one or more free accessories for its mid-price and luxury lines during special product promotion periods. Brand Z occasionally offers deep discounts for short periods, such as just prior to the Christmas holidays. Brand Z never offers free accessories and does not even offer accessories for its basic line of products.

ACME is currently tied for the number three position in the marketplace with Brand Z. Each company has a 12 percent share of the market. (Pease refer to the category review section for more details on the leading four competitors.)

ACME Company's business strategy is to compete in the market by offering the highest degree of quality, value, and craftsmanship. The company does not compete on price considerations. The business strategy is based on the assumption that consumers will pay a higher price for superior quality. ACME Company is sixteen years old. The first decade was a period of growth beginning with the basic unit and expanding through three tiers to the luxury unit. Accessories and color choices were introduced seven years ago.

The period of rapid expansion of product offerings has ended for the immediate future. Corporate management has made a decision to end expansion of the product line and to focus on improving quality, craftsmanship, and reliability of ACME's products. This decision is in keeping with the overall business philosophy of competing in the marketplace solely on the basis of superior quality and value to the consumer.

ACME's products are sold worldwide. Minor variations to the design of the products themselves, as well as to the design of the sales collateral materials, in-store display items, catalogs, and owners' manuals, have been made to satisfy various geographical requirements.

Market research has demonstrated that the ACME product line is not always perceived clearly by the consumer. During the product line's period of rapid expansion, particularly with the introduction of the luxury line, color choices, and accessories—the visual manifestation of the master brand—ACME was diluted and fragmented. Some consumers have complained that as they wish to add optional accessories, the packaging confuses them. They are not always sure that a particular accessory is compatible with their standard unit and its particular model year. ACME's three prime competitors make a claim that their accessories are compatible with—and superior to—ACME's accessories. These competitors often use the ACME name on their accessory packaging with a disclaimer, "Compatible with all ACME brand products." These competitors' accessories are priced much lower than ACME's accessories. In an attempt to alleviate this confusion, senior management at ACME Company has directed that the entire portfolio of product literature, packaging, in-store display units, and catalogs be redesigned to allow consumers to quickly and readily identify a "genuine ACME Company product." The ultimate goal is to ensure that the ACME brand is instantly identifiable by consumers, and that the business philosophy of ensuring the highest quality and value is clear to the various target audiences worldwide.

Notes: The company portfolio section is most valuable because it clearly defines the breadth of the project. In this example, the design team is able to succinctly convey what artifacts are to be redesigned, a description of each product, competitive product line components, and marketing and promotion techniques utilized by ACME and its competitors. This section also further explains ACME's management philosophy and business strategy.

A design team that is meeting to discuss this brief would undoubtedly want to make a large chart. Across the top, horizontally, I would suggest listing the components of the redesign: sales literature, in-store display, catalogs, packaging, and owners' manuals. Down the vertical axis, I would list each of the 100 SKUs described. The task would then be to discuss each item on the chart. If the first SKU listed in the vertical column was the full-size basic unit, and the first column in the horizontal unit was headlined "Sales Literature," the team would now have an area of focus for discussion. I would list the sales literature currently available for the full-size basic unit from ACME Company, then list the sales literature available from the other three competitors for their basic units. I would proceed in the same way for each SKU and each category in the redesign project. You can see this will be time-consuming—but at the same time, critical!

The result will be a giant matrix that will clearly show the overall scope of the work, the materials you will need to assemble for a visual audit, and the company's areas of strength and vulnerability. You will really need to do some exercise like this one prior to considering your overall design strategy. The project could be thought of as a giant jigsaw puzzle. You will need to assemble all of the pieces, then attempt to solve the puzzle in a coherent and logical manner.

This type of process will also be critical to creating detail for the description, time line, and budget for each phase.

If this particular project had been described only as a redesign of one tier, say, the luxury tier of products, you would probably want to do this complete exercise anyway. It does not make sense to redesign just one product, or one group of products, without understanding how these products fit with the rest of the company portfolio.

Now for some good news! Why not start right now to develop your own design group company portfolio chart? Why wait for a project to come along? I am aware of design groups in several companies that have done this as a matter of routine. These design groups tell me that just designing this company portfolio chart, and keeping it updated as new products are introduced and others are eliminated, has made an enormous difference in all of their design work.

One Fortune 500 company I have worked with constructed a special room for this kind of activity. Whole walls were covered with examples or photographs of each of their products, and the visual support materials for each product. Prime competitive material was integrated with their own materials. This had been the design group's idea and was primarily created as a design resource. However, as word about this room spread, people from just about every function in the company came to visit the display. Both marketing and sales said that it was the most useful company presentation they had ever seen. The CEO was ecstatic. Not a bad way to get positive recognition for design within the company, and save yourself an awful lot of time developing design brief content!

Business Objectives and Design Strategy

Business Objectives	Design Strategy
Restore visual cohesiveness and clarity to company portfolio of products in order to strengthen brand recognition among consumers.	Develop a unique grid system which will be used consistently with every application across all three tiers.
	Develop a standard typographic system that will be used consistently with every application.
	Develop a color palette that will be used consistently for all products. Explore concepts that will utilize specific color coding for each tier of products.
	Explore concepts that will utilize various forms of imagery to define products (e.g. photography, illustration, and image concepts that include people using the product, as well as concepts that feature the product only).
Ensure that ACME Company's products are clearly differentiated, visually, from all competitors.	Audit all major competitors for use of specific visual elements and style.
	Develop design concepts that are uniquely different from all competitors' while still communicating "superior quality."

Improve market share and the bottom line.	Develop design concepts which have the key objectives of making all products instantly recognizable as ACME brand products, make each tier attractive to the specific target audience for the particular tier, and powerfully reinforce the primary messages of superior quality and value.
Enhance equity in the ACME brand by maintaining corporate brand identity standards.	Develop design concepts that display the corporate logo prominently and consistently across the entire product line.
	Build on brand heritage by not altering the brand logo in any way, but also allowing the brand to appear more contemporary by utilizing the brand logo in more contemporary physical environments.
Establish design guidelines for the possibility of future new products being added to the company portfolio when the market recovers.	Develop design concepts that are representative of current fads or trends in design. Pursue design concepts that are more "classical" in approach without appearing "old-fashioned" or dated.
	Determine what types of new products might be anticipated, and what the target audience for these new products might be.
	Develop a design house style guide which could endure for at least ten years.
Clearly distinguish each value tier: • basic • basic commercial/ low end • mid-price • luxury models	Develop concepts that maintain a cohesive visual appearance of the brand across the entire company portfolio but still allowing for use of various individual graphic devices for each value tier.

Note: Please note that the design strategies listed do not specifically describe any particular design element or concept. Rather, this section simply lists those business objectives that the company feels are critical to the outcomes of this project and ensures that there is an agreed-upon design strategy for each one. As mentioned in Chapter 3, these design strategies may be changed as work begins on concept development. That's okay. This is simply a jumping-off point. The business objectives may also change. Usually, this takes the form of adding business objectives, not deleting them. If a business objective is added, it will more than likely alter some of the initial design strategies.

However, the goal is to minimize the number of changes, or—hopefully—to eliminate them altogether. The design strategies should be discussed with the design team prior to including them in the first draft of the design brief. As a possible exercise in your own design group, try taking the business objectives outlined in this list and seeing what design strategies your own group might come up with. More than likely, they will be different from the ones used in this example!

Project Scope, Time Line, and Budget

Note: In the following example, the design group is presumed to be an in-house corporate graphic design group that is centrally funded by the corporation. All graphic design staff are salaried employees; therefore, no budget has been assigned to this project for graphic design staff labor (time). Salaried employees are generally not eligible for overtime pay. In most instances, the centrally funded group's employee salary and benefit overhead is not charged back to specific design projects. If this project were to be executed by an external design firm, or an in-house group that operates on a charge-back system for staff time, employee overhead would have to be calculated into the project cost. Obviously, this would make the budget for the specific project a great deal higher.

- Phase 1—*Comprehensive visual audit of existing company portfolio, as well as a visual audit of the top three competitors' portfolios.* This phase will include:
  - Assembling one copy of each ACME Company catalog, unit of sales collateral literature, current in-store display unit, package, owner's manual, and product.

- Assembling one copy of each of the above for Brands X, Y, and Z. (Note: The corporate strategic design group already has all of this material from ACME Company and the competitors as it is gathered on a routine basis. Therefore, very little time will be required to assemble this material.)
- Design team to conduct a visual audit of all material listed. Time frame for this activity will be five full business days (forty hours). The strategic design manager and the four designers (names should be listed) will conduct this initial audit. Because of our funding structure, and because all materials are currently available, there is no direct cost to the project for this activity.
- The strategic design group shall prepare a written report of the findings from this audit. In particular, this report shall contain detailed information about how the audit results relate to the stated business objectives of this project, as well as the apparent strengths and weaknesses of the design elements utilized by Brands X, Y, and Z.

  The design audit results document shall be prepared by the strategic design manager, (name), and the lead designer of the design project team, (name). This audit report will require three business days to prepare. There is no cost to the project for development of this report, as the design function is centrally funded.
- Both hard copies and electronic copies of this report shall be distributed to the entire design team, the design brief project team, all previously identified project stakeholders, and all approvers who will be listed for each phase of the project. The completed visual audit report shall also become a part of the appendix of this design brief.

  Materials used for the visual audit shall be maintained by the strategic design group and made available to anyone within the company who wishes to review the material on his own. The cost of duplication, distribution (postage and handling by a document distribution company contracted by ACME Company), and storage of the materials will be $600. The report distribution company will require two business days for copying and distribution.

- The visual audit report will be reviewed by (name), co-owner/partner of the project (previously identified as the vice president of marketing), the vice president of sales, the international marketing director, and the entire design brief project team. A meeting of this entire team will be scheduled to review their comments and concerns six business days after the distribution of the report. At the conclusion of this meeting, the design brief project team will approve the visual audit document.
- The total time frame for this phase shall be seventeen business days (including the six business days for individual review by key stakeholders). The total cost for this phase will be $600.

- Phase 2—Develop a maximum of six creative design concepts that meet business objectives. Working as a team, four designers from the strategic design group, under the overall direction of the strategic design manager, will develop a maximum of six creative concepts for presentation to the design brief project team for approval. More than six creative design concepts will be explored, but only six will be selected for presentation. The selected concepts will all address the business objectives, the design strategy, and the results of the visual audit.

The development and refinement of six design concepts for presentation will require six weeks of time by the design team. Expenses for external vendors of supplies and materials for this concept development project will not exceed $50,000. Typical examples of these external expenses include photography, model-making (for in-store display units), supplies for graphic design work, and some travel, lodging, and per diem out-of-pocket expense reimbursements for the design staff, who may have to engage in some limited travel.

Key stakeholders who will be routinely consulted during this concept development process include representatives from sales, marketing, law, the various global geographies, market research, external vendors for printing, display fabrication, package engineering, and manufacturing.

At the conclusion of this initial concept development phase, the design team shall present the six concepts to the entire design brief project team for discussion and approval. Once the design brief project team has granted approval, we will proceed to the next phase.

Phase 2 will require six weeks of concept development time and one week for design brief project team discussion and approval. The total time for phase two is seven weeks. The total budget for phase two is $50,000.

- Phase 3—*Test all concepts with target audiences.* PDF files of the six approved design concepts will be sent to sales and marketing executives in all regions and geographies. When practical, models of display units will also be sent to these representatives. Each representative will be asked to show all six concepts to at least five people from the target audience for each tier. No information shall be given to the members of the target audience. They will only be asked, "Could you please give me your immediate reaction to each of these design treatments?"

  Verbal responses are all that is required. These should be recorded on audiotape for each interview. Target audience interviews should take no more than fifteen to twenty minutes for each person interviewed. The objective is to obtain top-of-mind immediate responses to each design concept from the target audience. Written and audiotape recorded responses should be sent to the strategic design director at (name and address). Company representatives shall have three weeks to complete these interviews. Transcripts of these test results will be added to the appendix of this design brief.

  The total time allotted to Phase 3 is four weeks: one week for distribution of materials and three weeks for interviews. The budget for Phase 3, including duplication and distribution of the materials, is $5,000.

- Phase 4—*Select three concepts and further refine each.* Retest all three with target audience. Based upon worldwide target audience testing of the initial six design concepts, the design brief project team, in collaboration with the design team, will select three design concepts for further refinement. The design team will require three weeks for this refinement process. The cost of this further refinement process will be $35,000. This budget will cover the same categories of items as described in Phase 2.

  Upon refining three of the original design concepts, all three will be tested in an identical manner as described in Phase 3. Once again, the testing process will require four weeks and an expenditure of $5,000 of the total budget. These test result transcripts will also be added to the appendix of this design brief.

  The total time for Phase 4 will be seven weeks, and the total budget for Phase 4 will be $40,000.

- Phase 5—*Select one concept, fully develop it, and perform final testing.* The results of the Phase 4 design concept testing will be analyzed and discussed by the design brief project team and the design team. One concept will be approved for final development and ultimate presentation to senior management for approval. The four members of the design team shall collaborate producing comprehensives and models for this design solution.

  Key stakeholders who will be involved in this Phase 5 work other than the design brief team include:

  - The law department for final legal review
  - A representative from marketing from each major geography worldwide
  - A representative from procurement
  - All external vendors who will manufacture or produce the components of the project

- A representative from sales for all major geographies
- A representative from the corporate distribution function
- A representative from the finance function, who shall produce a final accounting analysis for the project.

In addition to fully developing the selected graphic design concept by the design team, each key stakeholder will be accountable for producing a written plan for implementation of the project from his or her functional perspective:

- Sales and marketing will develop internal and external communication plans
- Procurement will begin the process of preparing vendor bids and awarding contracts
- The law department will prepare a written opinion concerning any legal issues
- Distribution will prepare a definitive plan for replacing existing materials in the distribution system with the new materials once they are available
- Finance will prepare a full financial report for the project, to be available at the time of presentation to senior management for final approval.

Phase 5 will require eight weeks to complete. The final design development process has been budgeted at $100,000. At the conclusion of the final development of a design solution, an external testing agency will be engaged to professionally test the solution with the target audience worldwide. The testing agency will be given four weeks for testing and preparing a report on the test results. The budget for external testing has been set at $100,000. The total time frame for Phase 5 is twelve weeks. The total budget, including the cost of testing, has been set at $200,000. The external agency test result summaries will be added to the appendix of this design brief.

At the conclusion of Phase 5, the design team, the external testing agency, and the entire design brief project team shall meet to formally approve the design solution. This meeting will be scheduled as a full-day meeting. One week prior to this meeting, all members of the design brief project team shall be sent PDF files of the design solution, the test results, and all formal written plans produced by additional key stakeholders. This will allow the design brief project team to attend the final approval meeting with substantive knowledge of the entire plan, as well as the business rationale for the approval of the final design solution that the team previously selected.

- Phase 6—*Develop approval presentation.* The co-owners of the project shall be accountable for preparing a senior management approval presentation and for making this presentation to (name) on (date and time). The design team shall prepare all visual artifacts for this approval presentation. The final approver will be sent all materials, including the design brief and all reports from key stakeholders, one week prior to the final approval presentation.

  The co-owners of the project will require two weeks for preparation of this approval presentation. The budget for the development and production of the approval presentation is $8,000.
- Phase 7—*Implement approved design solution.* In order to implement the approved new design concept for the entire project line in a short period of time, a subcommittee of the design brief project team shall be formed to develop an implementation plan.

  This plan shall include specific instructions for rapid liquidation of current supplies of printed collateral sales literature, catalogs, owners' manuals, and packaging. Additionally, this plan will include the consumer communications plan and a new sales and marketing plan for the rollout, in addition to describing any variations required by different geographies. The implementation plan shall become an integral part of the senior management's final approval presentation. This detailed implementation plan will be developed during the same time period as the final approval presentation as described in Phase 6 (total time two weeks). Since each of the corporate functions will develop its portion of the implementation plan individually, no budget has been assigned to this activity.

The goal is to achieve full worldwide implementation of the new company portfolio design within one business quarter (three months). Manufacturing and distribution of the new materials, as well as disposal of the current manifestations of all artifacts, is estimated to cost $1,000,000.

- Phase 8—Develop measurement metrics. Based upon the stated and approved business objectives for this project, measurement metrics have been developed by the design brief project team. (Name of company) has been contracted to conduct monthly surveys by telephone of typical customers worldwide. Twelve hundred customers and prospective customers will be contacted each month. These surveys will continue for a period of two years. Results of each monthly survey will be made available to the design brief project team and ACME senior management on a monthly basis.

  These surveys will measure reaction to a standard group of questions designed to determine: unaided awareness of the ACME brand, unaided awareness of Brands X, Y, and Z; recall and understanding of key messages and reasons to buy, as put forth by the aforementioned competitors as well as by ACME Company, and likelihood of a preference for each of these brands. The complete questionnaire and specific details concerning this testing are included in the appendix of this design brief. Key findings will address the following questions:

  - Is the ACME brand clear to members of the target audience for each product line tier?
  - What percentage of the target audience recognizes and is aware of the ACME brand?

- How do consumers differentiate the offerings of the top four brands in the market?
- Do consumers easily recognize the different value tiers through visual means?
- How long has each respondent been aware of the ACME brand?
- Has the respondent's opinion of the ACME brand changed in any way over the past year?

ACME's finance group and investor relations will continue to track sales and revenue results worldwide on a monthly basis, as well as changes in stock price. However, over this same two-year period, these results will also be incorporated into the monthly company portfolio redesign project measurement reports.

Product research and development teams will closely monitor the approved future design standards and guidelines for new products as developed for this project. Any element of the new standards and guidelines that becomes difficult to incorporate will be brought to the attention of the strategic design manager immediately. The design brief project team shall continue to meet on a monthly basis with representatives of senior management to discuss and evaluate these monthly reports.

The total time frame to complete this project to the point of implementation is thirty-four and one half weeks (8.6 months). The total budget for this project is $303,600. Implementation worldwide will cost $1,000,000.

Note: There you have it—a complete road map for the project. This section is also a useful project tracking device, a formal agreement between all parties, an educational tool for your non-design partners, and a terrific way to demonstrate design is a complex, strategic process.

This example was based upon a major activity for any company—the complete redesign of its entire company portfolio. Therefore, the cost undoubtedly seems very high to you. It probably would seem high to senior management as well! But, by breaking the activities and costs down by phases, it becomes difficult to disagree with the numbers. What activity could senior management possibly eliminate for a project with such high stakes—the ultimate survival of the company in its category? It might also be interesting for you to think about what this project would cost if the price of design labor had been factored in. This is another reason I strongly advocate that in-house corporate design groups be centrally funded. The cost of each employee for the year remains the same to the company whether they do one or two major projects or one hundred smaller ones. Of course, smaller projects than the one in this example would be described very differently. Again, that is why I keep saying each design brief will be unique. It must be developed for a particular project for a particular company. I chose this kind of example because I wanted to include a wide variety of issues that I had discussed earlier.

I'd also like to point out the efficiencies a design group can offer if you routinely assemble competitive materials and build a company portfolio matrix of your own. Ultimately, it will save you a great deal of time, and senior management will be very impressed with your group.

I suspect many readers will argue that there is an awful lot of testing called for in this design brief. They would tell me that their management wouldn't allow all that time and money for testing. For reasons I have already covered earlier in this book, testing is what will allow a corporation, and its design group (whether internal or external), to know whether they are on the right track or not. In my career, when I encountered resistance to all the testing I was recommending, I would simply ask senior management how much time it would take and how much more would it cost, if we implemented a new design and the target audience reacted negatively. Would we have the time and money to do it all over again? Usually they had to agree, especially on high-visibility projects such as the one in this example. If you are asked to do a project that is considerably lower in risk, you would probably not have the time and money to do such extensive testing. In those cases, I would simply do my own informal testing, as described earlier. I would personally visit a dozen or so customers in the company of a salesperson making routine sales calls, and get some reactions from customers by myself. No matter what, I would want some target audience input.

Research Data

The primary missing research data for this project includes an R&D forecast for the types of new products under development (or planned at this time), the approximate timing of their introduction, and the market analysis and target audience demographics and description for these new products. This information will be critical to the development of the graphic design standards, guidelines, principles, and strategies for future new products. The graphic design team will not be able to develop a comprehensive plan without this data.

(Name) from R&D and (name) from the market research group will be accountable to provide this data to the strategic design manager no later than (date). Additionally, the finance group will agree to do a cost-benefit analysis for this entire project based upon the costs budgeted in this design brief. This report will be prepared by (name) and presented to the design brief team no later than four weeks following the start of work on this project. This report will be made available to (name of final approver) by this same date.

Note: There is really not a great deal of missing research data in this excerpt. As mentioned, there are many times when no data is missing; in those cases, this section may be deleted.

This example of a design brief did not include much about those standards and guidelines for new products mentioned in the project overview and background section. This is because critical research data is missing. It doesn't mean the project cannot begin. It simply means that about a third of the way through the various phases this data will become necessary to complete the project. People have been identified to supply the data, and a date has been established. This is okay for now. If the data is not supplied in a timely manner, there is a written record in the design brief that it was required. This eliminates that old excuse, "If you had only told me sooner you would need this information. . . ." It's a matter of record now.

Finally, the cost-benefit analysis is mentioned. Prior to having an approved design brief, costs were only estimated. More than likely, the costs were underestimated! Now that the design brief team knows how much the project will really cost, it is wise to ensure that the investment is worthwhile. Additionally, this financial analysis will be of enormous help to you in preparing your approval presentation, and in the measurement process after the new design solution has been implemented. Alerting the final approver now is politically correct. You don't want that person to faint when you go in for final approval and he asks, "How much did this cost?" If there is going to be a problem, better to get it out in the open now, before you have gone very far.

Appendix

The appendix will be updated weekly as new material is completed. Contents include:

- Report of visual audit of ACME Company's portfolio, as well as of Brands X, Y, and Z.
- Results of Phase 3 global concept testing.
- Results of Phase 4 global concept testing.
- Executive summaries of external testing agency findings for global tests of recommended final design solution.
- Complete copy of final approval presentation.
- Complete copies of project implementation plans written and approved by various corporate functions, as described in Phase 7.
- Project cost-benefit analysis from corporate finance group.
- Copy of R&D new product development plans.
- Copy of market research new product market analysis and audience demographics.
- Measurement metrics questionnaires, plus monthly executive summary reports.

- PDF files of all major concepts initially explored by the graphic design group.
- Competitive materials and data.

Note: As mentioned before, the appendix becomes a collection of "stuff" that really doesn't fit anywhere else. The whole design brief, including all of the material in the appendix, will become valuable archival material for future projects. Creating great design briefs actually becomes easier and faster with each one you develop. Very often, materials from one project will be absolutely essential to another project. Why keep reinventing the wheel? Archive your design briefs.

CHAPTER 8

Managing an In-House Graphic Design Staff

WE HAVE ALREADY GIVEN CONSIDERATION to the fact that many in-house, corporate graphic design staffs have been conditioned to be "taxi drivers." "Tell me where you want to go, and I will take you there." Many groups have also been conditioned to feel like nothing more than a service provider who is first and foremost trying to please people.

The primary purpose of this book is to reposition in-house graphic design functions from a drop-in service center to a core strategic business partner in the company.

The job of managing this transition is a formidable one. But the repositioning is only half the story. The staff of the in-house graphic design group will also have to go through a major change in mindset, as well as behavior. This new way of thinking, doing things, and behaving will likely cause many on your staff considerable anxiety. It will be a major change for them. As the design manager, or director of design, it will be your job to pay particular attention to the transition needs of your staff.

Graphic Design Professionals Are Unique

Over the years I have become firmly convinced that people who are driven to become graphic designers are a unique bunch. Their professional training, temperament, emotional needs, and sensitivity are different from many other employees of the company. They march to a different drummer. Often, it is this uniqueness that has made other folks in the company become a bit apprehensive of graphic designers.

I have attended numerous workshops, classes, and seminars over the years focused on "management." I have learned many valuable lessons from these classes, but none of them really addressed the unique needs of graphic designers.

Our very best graphic designers are *creative* people. They have an innate compulsion to create something fresh, and they are more than willing to work hard to reach that goal. Creative people, by nature, do not want to be boxed in—stifled. They need quite a bit of freedom to allow creativity to flourish. They need an environment which allows them to be creative. And, they need to feel comfortable about the possibility of making mistakes.

Although it is not as common today as it once was, many large corporations have failed to see this need for creative people to be—well, creative.

I recall a company vice president who dropped by my office to tell me that he saw several of my designers just looking out the window. He wanted to know why they weren't working hard to meet some tight deadlines. To him, nose to the grindstone was the only way to go. He really didn't want to hear about "thinking," "conceptualizing,' looking for "inspiration," etc. His take on the whole thing was that if you come to the office and get paid a day's wage, then you spend the day actually doing tangible things.

The Design Process

The graphic design process is not all about doing tangible things. The process is more about discovering exciting visual solutions to difficult business problems. Often, this may include a fair amount of trial and error. How many times have you, as a graphic designer, come up with a concept which seems likely to work well, but, as you develop and push this concept it becomes clear that it really isn't working to solve the problem? It becomes necessary to begin again with another concept.

I am flattered to learn that many non-designers really believe we can go into some back room and magically emerge shortly with a brilliant design solution. I have heard, and I am sure you have too, "Hey guy, work your magic on this one!" Unfortunately magic is not what we do. Great design solutions require heavy duty thinking, more than a little trial and error, skill, talent, training, and experience. Non-designers (who believe we are some kind of "artist") really do not understand the design process very well.

One marketing executive in a company I was part of actually said to me, “Come on, it doesn’t have to be all that great. I don’t need award winning design, I just need the brochure done!” He expected to see, at least something, the next day. The gentleman had no idea of the process we have to use to develop an effective design solution.

Nearly every graphic design professional I have ever met has expressed frustration with their business partners who, “Just don’t get it.” It is my belief that the real problem is not with our non-design partners. The problem lies within the graphic design profession. We, in this profession, have not done a very good job of communicating our process, in understandable terms, to our non-design colleagues. We need to do a better job of managing our communications.

The Climate Needed for In-House Graphic Design

It will be very important to establish the correct climate and environment, for your in-house graphic design group.

The graphic designers need to feel safe in this environment. They will need to feel empowered to work the graphic design process the way it needs to be worked. They will need to feel it is okay to experiment, to explore concepts, to toss ideas around with each other. It is the responsibility of the design manager to be sure this climate exists within the company. The manager has to become a type of buffer between the best graphic design process or processes and the design group’s business partners who use totally different processes for their work.

I did some consulting work, not that long ago, for a graphic design group which was part of a very large, and very old, well-established, United States Corporation. The company had rather strict standards with regard to office space and behavior within the walls of the corporate headquarters.

For example, the size of an employee’s work space (cubical) was arrived at by a factor based upon the employee’s grade (salary). All employees in the company of a similar grade, had exactly the same size cubicle. One size fits all, in any particular salary grade! Unfortunately, these small cubicles did not in any way provide the space, or climate, necessary for graphic designers to effectively do their work. The design manager had tried, several times, to request a change in this policy for his group. He had not been successful.

One of the things I was asked to help with was to get some relief for the in-house graphic design group from this "space" policy.

My solution was to develop a presentation for management which explained not only the process of design, and the tools graphic designer's need to do their work, but also the ultimate *financial benefit to the company* of utilizing this process. I kept the language of my presentation very businesslike, and avoided any design jargon. The entire focus was on the benefit to the *company* not just the benefit to the design group. It worked!

It worked for several reasons. First, it was about the benefits for the *company.* Next, it was educational for non-designers; they finally began to have a real world grasp of graphic design process. I was also able to make the presentation to a higher level of management than the in-house manager had been able to reach on his own. This was, in part, possible because I was a credentialed external consultant. A prophet is seldom heard in his own land!

In the end, the company did benefit from exempting design from the salary determines space standard. We made sure of that by building in measurement metrics to the presentation. The metrics were business based, and quantifiable. We developed metrics based on measurable volume of output for the department, average time to complete strategic projects, and a number of efficiency metrics.

What this change process was really all about was a compelling communication about the process of graphic design, and the added value of design to the company's bottom line.

Making Sure Your Graphic Design Staff Is "On-Board" with Becoming a Core Strategic Competency

Up until this point, we have assumed your entire in-house graphic design group really wants to leave the service center mode and to become strategic partners with non-designers. To one extent or another, this may be partially true. There will be some members of your group who will be very eager to move ahead. But, most likely, you will also have some of your staff feeling a bit nervous about making such a dramatic change. Some may even feel that such a change is really not going to be possible for them. They may have had long-term relationships with people in the company as a service provider. They will probably feel all of these strategic partner changes will negatively affect these former relationships. Others may feel that, quite frankly, they just won't be able to work and "partner" this way. It hasn't been part of their training or past experience.

In one of my workshops on this topic, a gentleman said to the group, "I would love to see all of this become a reality in my company. My problem is that I have a few designers that have been with the group nearly twenty years. They won't want to change the way they have been working for so long. What do I do? Fire them?"

Absolutely not!

The longevity, and also the extensive history and knowledge of the company of these long-term employees is something to value. You don't want to lose this experience. Your job, as design manager, is to factor into your plans the reality that not everyone in your group will be capable of, or interested in, becoming a strategic partner. This is okay. What you will need to do is focus on each of your staff members. Determine their individual strengths and weaknesses. Several will be well suited to the role of becoming a strategic partner with non-design business partners. And so, these folks will be the primary people to fill this role. Others, who either do not want to change the way they have been working, or who, for a variety of reasons, are just not comfortable in the partner role, need to be assigned to the projects they can handle best. I assigned one graphic designer in a former group of mine who fit this description of not really wanting the strategic partner role to become Manager of the Design Production Group. I didn't terminate this employee; I promoted her. She did an amazing job in this role. Of course, you can't have more than one Design Production Unit Manager. But since you now have a good grip on the types of projects that will flow through your group, you will need to assign projects carefully according to various people's interest and abilities. Many production-focused design projects that you have opted to continue handling in-house will not require heavy-duty strategic partnering. Assign these projects appropriately. Some of your staff will be greatly relieved.

Also keep in mind, if someone has been with your group twenty or more years, they are probably looking toward retirement in a few years. Once they do retire, or move on to another job, your job will be to fill those vacancies with designers who are comfortable in the strategic partner role.

Industry studies indicate graphic designers today rarely stay with the same company for twenty years. In fact, the averages are more like five to seven years. Then they move on for fresh challenges. What this means to a design manager is that the process of evaluating the design skills you really need in your department is a constant process.

The Importance of Becoming a Mentor

Most design professionals I know don't really need to be "managed" as much as they need to be "led." You, the design manager, are the leader. This means you need to take a real leadership role in this repositioning effort. You must be ready to listen to your staff's concerns, suggestions, and, possibly, fears. You need to lead your staff from a business-as-usual mode to an exciting new and refreshing valued partner role. Just as you will need to carefully communicate your repositioning to the company as a whole, you will also need to carefully communicate the new positioning to your design staff. The very best way is to involve each and every member of your staff at every step of the process. Allow your staff as a group to discuss all of the possibilities. Listen to their ideas. Listen to their concerns. Let them know you are all in this together. It is not your project; this repositioning project is a group effort.

Your job, as the leader of this group effort is to cause people to:

- Know what to do, when to do it, and how to do it.
- Know how their individual work adds value to the design function and to the goals of the company as a whole.
- Understand, clearly, what criteria will be used to measure the success of the group, as well as their individual contributions.

- Make sure they feel challenged and personally accountable for their design solutions.
- Make sure they feel supported, as members of a smoothly functioning graphic design team.
- Make sure they really feel that the company encourages, values, and recognizes their personal competence.
- Make sure they feel it is safe and okay to speak up, and have their ideas and points of view heard.
- Make sure they anticipate success and the rewards associated with success.

Being a mentor means helping each of your staff with all of the above.

Professional Development

In most of the management workshops and seminars I attended in the past, some emphasis was put on counseling employees to explore different parts of the company. For instance, spend a year in the field as a salesperson; work in the marketing department for a period of time; learn more about the finance function; and so forth. The intention was to "develop" a good employee by having him or her acquire a wide variety of skills. It is my belief that graphic designers do not want or need this broad development program. People who are professional graphic designers want to do just that—great graphic design. Usually they do not aspire to rise through the ranks to eventually become a Vice-President of some function in the company. Graphic designers are specialists. Graphic design is the only profession they want. As a matter of fact, many really talented designers do not want the job of design manager either!

It is my belief that graphic design professionals have to be "developed" in different ways. Rather than have them spend a year or so in the field as a salesperson, they should attend sales meetings occasionally as spectators. As mentioned earlier in this book, I would send my designers out for a day or two with sales people to watch them use the sales materials our graphic design group had created. The goal was not to make them sales people; the goal was to expose them, occasionally, to actual selling situations. None of my staff ever came back from a day in the field, or a sales meeting, and told me they wanted to switch careers and become a sales person.

Graphic designers do need professional development—but in the graphic design profession. There are many design conferences, design workshops and seminars, and even formal college extension courses, which would be beneficial for your designers. Try to get a decent professional development budget and then spend some time determining which events would be most useful for each of your design staff. Trust me; they will deeply appreciate these opportunities. It is very important for graphic designers to get out and mingle with others in the graphic design profession. It is possible to become very isolated by just staying in the corporate shop all the time, and that is not healthy.

CHAPTER 9

Motivating Your Graphic Design Staff

THERE SEEMS TO BE MANY definitions of "motivation." A former teacher of mine said: "Motivation is the reason why you behave the way you do." Another educator said: "Motivation is having the willingness to go over the top in order to excel." One definition, which I relate to personally, is: "Motivation means to incite, or give good cause to another individual to do something."

No matter how you care to define motivation in specific words, motivation is all about making people really want to do, or accomplish, something.

Much has been written, and taught, about Maslow's hierarchy of needs model, and Herzberg's motivator-hygiene model. More than likely you are aware of these two models already, so I will not dwell on them in this book.

In brief, Maslow's need-hierarchy deals with:

- Physiological Needs
- Safety and Security
- Belonging and Affiliation
- Self-esteem
- Self-actualization

Herzberg's Motivator-Hygiene Model focuses on:

- Work itself achievement
- Responsibility
- Recognition and Advancement
- Status
- Interpersonal Relations
- Supervision—Technical
- Company Policy and Administration
- Job Security
- Working Conditions
- Salary
- Personal Life

I have no arguments or problems with either Maslow's or Herzberg's theories. For me, all of the above are critical for a variety of reasons. I must admit Maslow's list more closely matches the needs of graphic design professionals. Why are all these theories so necessary for a design manager to understand? Well, for starters they provide a coherent framework for analyzing the behaviors of your graphic design staff. Using that framework the design manager is better able to identify dominant motives of his or her staff. All of this will help the design manager lead the graphic design staff in a way that will further arouse and satisfy these dominant motives, resulting in higher levels of group performance.

You Must Understand Personalities

All of us are blessed (in some cases, cursed) with an individual personality. These various personalities all have needs. These needs will have to be met in order for a particular personality to be truly motivated.

David McClelland did research and wrote extensively on this subject. You can Google him to find a list of his books and articles. Basically, he developed a "Three Social Motive" concept. I have always found McClelland's concepts more useful for managing graphic designers than other concepts. For me it has been more useful because it is more objective than philosophical. His concepts deal with everyday, observable speech and behavior. Finally, they are sound concepts based upon scientific fact, not pie-in-the-sky theories. McClelland's teachings really do work.

McClelland teaches that different personalities have different needs. There are a great many varieties of these needs, but three are dominant.

- Need for Achievement
- Need for Affiliation
- Need for Power

All of the other various needs we each have fall under these key three personality needs.

McClelland states that we all have the three needs, but depending on our personality, one of them will be dominant. In order to determine the best way to motivate an individual, it will first be necessary to identify his or her personality's dominant need. Let's look at them one at a time.

Need for Achievement

The need for achievement is the personality's need to excel or do very well in a particular task, as indicated by:

- Outperforming someone else (competitive)
- Meeting or exceeding a self-imposed standard of excellence (internal competition)
- Significant concern for unique accomplishments
- Concern for achieving long-term objectives
- Concern about, and plans for, overcoming personal and technical obstacles

We all know people with this personality type and needs. Persons, whose need for achievement is high, look for challenge. They also look for competition. They set objectives which are difficult but which represent the possibility of success. They have a concern for accuracy and quality. They like to plan. They are constantly planning their next move.

Over the course of my career I have had several great strategic graphic designers in my groups who were driven by this need. They were highly competitive in everything they did in their lives. They were easy to spot, often their work space was adorned with awards and trophies they had won, framed letters from various people who had praised their work, photos of them with important people, etc. Once you have identified particular designers with this strong need for achievement, you can begin devising a personalized plan for motivating them to excel in their work. It is wise to create challenges for them both short and long term. Then reward them in some way when the challenges are met.

You might enter some of their work in design competitions, or you might write an article about one of their design accomplishments for the company newsletter. In their performance review you could spend some time with them on goal setting, and planning to help them overcome some obstacle. Perhaps they are not comfortable making one-on-one or group presentations. You might suggest some workshops or seminars which might help them excel in this area. And, of course, these employees will become highly motivated by being openly praised when praise is warranted. It never hurts to say to an achievement personality, "We could never have done it without you!" Not to say all of your graphic designers do not need praise, but these achievement driven personalities will become highly motivated by this praise. They need to know they have achieved!

Need for Affiliation

The dominant need of an affiliation-driven personality is the need to establish, maintain, or restore positive emotional relationships with other people as indicated by:

- Concern for people in both work and non-work settings
- Characterization of many settings as social situations
- Concern about being accepted, liked, and having friends

The people in your group with these dominant personality needs can be somewhat difficult to motivate. They will be very concerned about attaining objectives that have to do with establishing, maintaining, and repairing personal contacts and relationships. These people will be the ones who will be reluctant to "rock the boat" and change their behavior. If they have been in service-provider mode for a long time, they may feel changing what has been a good relationship with the people requesting their graphic design services may jeopardize those good relationships. This will cause them to be anxious about change.

Affiliation personalities abhor confrontation. They need to be liked! You will probably notice they tend to decorate their work space with family photos, photos of their pets, and warm, friendly colors.

I know a CEO who is a big time affiliation personality. Whenever he speaks to a group of employees he emphasizes, "We are a family here at XYZ Company. Our customers love us. Even our competitors like us." His secret nickname among employees is "Grandpa." Whenever anything goes wrong, he says, "Don't worry, we can work it all out, after all we are a family, we are together in all of this."

The best way to motivate an affiliation personality is to emphasize how much our "partners" will appreciate our efforts. How much more they will like us when things start moving along more smoothly. That being a partner rather than service provider will bring us even closer together than before. Once they understand that personal relationships can and will improve, they will become more motivated to nurture the partnership concept. Affiliation personalities enjoy socializing, so engage in a little social conversation with them every week. Also provide ample opportunities for them to work in pairs, groups, or committees. Send a winter holiday greeting card to them and their families!

Affiliation personalities enjoy hearing things like, "When your business partner sees this solution you have created, they will love it."

Need for Power

Personalities which are driven by a need for power need to have strong influence on, or control over others, as indicated by:

- Always taking strong action
- Strong concerns for symbols of power
- Concern for arousing strong emotional reactions (positive or negative) in others
- Concern for resisting territorial encroachment by others

The power personalities demonstrate a concern for attaining objectives related to gaining and exercising "influence" or "control." This personality type is apt to be more forceful than others in trying to be persuasive. They enjoy impressing others. Often they will offer unasked-for advice, assistance, or support. This personality type is stimulated by debate or argument and takes great satisfaction in "winning the debate."

The power personality enjoys displaying symbols of their power. They become very concerned about decorating their work space with these symbols. Expensive items, fine art, exclusive club membership certificates, advanced degree diplomas. Often they will want to drive expensive automobiles, and wear expensive clothing. Another CEO I met was a classic power personality. He would only wear Armani silk suits. He was extremely fastidious. He had requested his business cards be printed on very thin stock. He always carried exactly ten business cards in his suit jacket side pocket. He needed the thin stock in order to assure there would be no apparent bulge from the cards in his pocket. He had plant maintenance shorten the conference table next to his office so he would not have to wear his eyeglasses in a meeting. He was extremely particular, all to make a powerful statement about his status in the company.

The power personality is sensitive about his or her "territory." This could be resentment about sharing a work space or an administrative assistant. They fully expect instant access to other people when they feel that is necessary for them.

The best ways to motivate a power personality is to monitor their progress on projects and provide feedback which does not threaten their self-esteem, reputation, or position. If you can, find ways to provide them with public recognition. Allow these folks some opportunities to assume a leadership role as chairperson of a department committee, or to represent you, the manager, at some event. When possible, stress the importance of their contributions in achieving departmental goals or objectives. Be aware of their "territorial" hang-ups. Resolve conflicts about territory quickly and fairly so no one loses face. Solicit their input on important decisions the department needs to make. If realistic, give them several high-profile, high prestige graphic design projects. Finally, you will be able to motivate power personalities just by introducing them to high status people in your company.

A Few General Thoughts about Motivation

The preceding paragraphs focused on motivating three specific personality types. But there are some more generalized motivation techniques to consider.

As design manager of an extremely busy design function, you probably feel overwhelmed with the workload. Many design managers have said to me, "There just isn't enough time to do everything I'm supposed to do as a manager." Welcome to the real world. Every manager I have ever met says the same thing. The issue here is time management on your part. You are probably not really Superman or Superwoman. You will need to take some time to evaluate all that you have on your plate. It will be a full plate, so look for ways to delegate some of your daily tasks to others. This can be particularly motivating to graphic designers on your staff. The boss trusts me enough to deal with this issue (whatever it might be), and get back to him or her with some results. Delegation, accompanied by full explanation of the issue, will make your staff feel more empowered and valued. It will also take some of the load off your daily routine.

Mix and mingle. Today, a design manager cannot simply sit in his or her office most of the day, or attend endless meetings. You must find time for your staff. You need to reach out to each staff member each day, even if for only a few minutes. Check in with them daily and let them know you care about what they are working on, and that you care about them personally. Again, this will be motivating. I know of a design manager that made a point of having lunch with a different member of his staff every day. Even if the lunch was taken in the manager's office with take-out from the cafeteria. The staff appreciated the frequent one-on-one contact with the boss, and everyone has to eat!

Use these one-on-one few minutes with each staff member each week to not simply ask for a status report on their project(s), but also to *consult* with them. Ask them for their input on some departmental issue. Then be sure to listen to their input and thank them for it.

Frequently remind your staff of their added value to the company.

Offer your staff perks such as professional development opportunities, ability for them to attend design conferences and seminars, and opportunities to attend a trade show or international sales meeting once in awhile.

If you have regular staff meetings, make them interesting, not simply a series of project status reports. Think about occasionally bringing in a guest to speak to them for ten or fifteen minutes about activities going on in other parts of the company.

Finally, vary their project load so they do not burn out by doing the same thing every day. One of my former design staff told me he had been doing the design for a particular brand's promotional material for thirteen years. He obviously had extensive knowledge about the brand, but he was burning out. I moved him to another brand. His motivation increased dramatically just by having a new challenge.

Physical Environment

Physical environment can play an enormous role in not only motivating your staff, but also in making your department more efficient and productive. Every time I visit a corporate design group (and I can count over 150 visits in the last five years) the design manager wants to take me on a tour of the department. With very few exceptions, they all look alike. Rows of cubicles, usually gray, and an occasional large central area with work tables and other "designer stuff." If I walk through other areas of the company, they all look exactly alike. Rarely do I find cubicles abutting windows on the outside walls. There are corridors along the windows. This is usually done so no employee has a favored location.

Okay, I will go out on a limb here. Personally I believe this sameness is very un-motivating to a creative, graphic design group. The physical environment is usually too small, too bland, very unimaginative, stifling, and probably very economical for the corporation. It may seem not important enough, but I encourage design managers to do everything possible to have permission for the design function to design its own work space—without breaking the bank, of course. When I have visited independent design agencies, I usually see very creative work environments for designers and "creatives." These areas are not necessarily lavish or even "artsy." They are simply comfortable spaces wherein designers can create their own décor and environment to do their work. They also tend to be a bit more "roomy" than traditional office spaces.

For me, physical environment can be very motivational for designers, particularly, and possibly very helpful to improved productivity for the company.

Finally, the very best motivator is to be sure you hire graphic designers who have a real passion for their work and the profession of graphic design.

CHAPTER 10

Scheduling the Workload

IN CHAPTER 4, I DESCRIBED a method of clearing some of the small, relatively minor, non-strategic graphic production projects out of your department. Although this will help enormously by getting rid of some project clutter, it will most likely still leave you with a rather large project load. A common plea I have heard in my consulting work is, "How do I schedule all of the work we have to do in a more efficient way?"

Unfortunately, there is no one-size-fits-all solution. Each graphic design group's situation will be different depending on the size of the group, the number and types of projects the group is expected to handle, and the available skill sets in your group. You, the manager of the group, must first do an intensive analysis of your situation.

I would suggest starting with the work itself. In Chapter 4 I suggested you go back two or three years and list all of the projects that flowed through your group. Hopefully, you were able to eliminate many of these projects by coming up with a system to send them to an external production house. But now you have a list of typical workloads your group will still be handling in-house.

The next step would be to determine if there are any projects that arrive at a certain, specified time of the year—for example, if your company publishes an updated product catalog every October. Determine if there are scheduled trade shows, sales meetings, new product introductions, or annual sales such as January clearance sales. Some consumer product companies schedule special offers around events such as Back to School, Father's Day or Mother's Day, Christmas and so forth. Develop a list of known events, and the dates of these events, which will require graphic design from your department for the coming year. This will give you a list of "knowns" to begin developing a month-by-month staff scheduling plan. Of course there will be a great many unknowns as well, but you cannot make a list of unknowns! What you should be able to do is arrive at an average number of unknowns that historically flow through your graphic design group annually. It won't be exact, of course, but it will give you a starting point.

Many corporations require brand or product marketing groups to submit a detailed forecast of strategies, new product introductions, and special events, etc., for the coming year. If you are fortunate enough to work in a company that has this requirement, make sure your business partners copy you on these marketing plans. It will help immensely in your own workload planning for the coming year.

The next step in this process is to honestly analyze the skill sets you have available in your group. Looking at the lists you have just made, try to match projects to the skill sets you have available. From there, the fun begins! It is not unusual to get this far and determine that certain skill sets in your group will be way overloaded. This is where the advance planning for the year comes back. Let's say you have one strategic graphic designer whose skills are perfect for trade show collateral, sales meeting support material, and special events such as holiday product sales. And, let's say many of these events will occur at roughly the same time. It will be immediately clear this one graphic designer will never be able to handle such a load in a specific time period. What will be necessary is to select a few projects in that known time period and pre-assign the projects most in need of a particular graphic designer's skills and strengths. For the other projects in that time frame, you will have to consider which of your remaining graphic designers would be best to assign those projects to.

I realize that many graphic design groups assign specific designers to specific brands or product lines. There are a great many advantages to this system. For one, the graphic designer gets an in-depth understanding of the brand or product, and its history. Another advantage is often excellent working relationships have been established between the brand or product managers and the graphic designer. All-in-all it is an excellent system. But, if your workload is such that you have more projects than your graphic designers can sanely handle, it might be necessary to rethink your process. I have personally managed both types of process: dedicated assignment to brand or product line, and the more open scheduling technique of assigning by skill sets and timing. For a long time I was a real advocate of the dedicated graphic designer to a product line or brand, for all the reason's listed above. But, as I mentioned, the graphic designer who had been dedicated to a particular brand for thirteen years was burning out. When I moved him to become a "floater," assigning him only to projects that really needed his particular skills, his attitude, motivation, and productivity improved dramatically. The brand didn't want to lose him. They had a great working relationship. I assured the brand manager he would still be working on projects for their brand, which required his specific knowledge of the brand and his particular skills. It was just that he would no longer be their exclusive "go-to guy." The brand manager was not happy. However, my graphic designer was more motivated, productive, and happy to have a chance for some variety in his projects. The graphic designers that occasionally would get one of this brand's design projects were equally as delighted and motivated. One of them told me she had had some ideas for the brand for a long time and wanted very much to work with them. In a relatively short time all parties became more comfortable with the change. The brand still had access to their long-time partner. Other graphic designers executing projects for the brand also had ample access to the former brand-dedicated graphic designer for advice, counsel, and history. The brand still got some great graphic design, and the results of that design were positive. Often, a pair of new eyes may refresh an existing brand. In the end it all worked out very well. All of this made my scheduling of workloads more efficient as well. I began to highly favor the latter system. With the enormous increases I have seen in in-house graphic design group's workloads, I am now convinced the former "graphic designer dedicated to a particular product line" system is no longer a viable alternative. Graphic design is now being recognized as a core competency for companies. This is a two-edged sword, at best. One, graphic design is being valued more, and two, that tends to increase the project load.

Once I moved to scheduling graphic designers by matching skill sets to projects and time frames, the whole process of scheduling graphic designer's time was much easier for my group. When I could foresee a major problem of not enough in-house resources in a particular time frame, I would plan ahead to bring in a graphic design contractor for a short period of time to meet the demand for graphic design projects. Partnering with Procurement, we identified a few qualified graphic design contractors who could be on call during specific time periods. In time, these contractors would be able to handle a variety of projects since we took the time to educate them on our needs, design philosophy, and our processes.

The Unknown Projects

Now to the really difficult part—namely, all those projects that seem to pop up out of nowhere! There will always be such projects. Most of the time, the business rationale for these sudden graphic design needs are valid ones. I will work with my business partners to the very best of my ability to meet these legitimate needs. But I do draw the line somewhat when the real business rationale is lacking. Often when I have asked for the business rationale (need) for the project, I have heard statements like, "My boss is just tired of the current brochure, and he has directed that we replace it with a new one right away." To me that is not a valid business reason to immediately disrupt my already over-burdened graphic design staff, have them drop everything, and produce a new brochure immediately. In cases like this, I would tactfully explain that we would schedule the design of a new brochure as soon as possible after my business partner and I had collaborated on a design brief for the new brochure. If we need to design a new brochure, we need to be sure it is far superior to what already exists, and that the new design has very specific business purposes and objectives for the marketplace. I didn't say no. I didn't say it was not necessary. I simply said the project needed to be carefully planned in order to achieve the most benefit to the company. Then we could commit time, money, and human resources to the project. By presenting a viable, business-like plan to the product group, I (usually) won the day.

But what do you do when you do not win the day? What happens when the executive demanding the new brochure has a powerful position and allies in the company? I hate to bring this up, but sometimes you have to face the reality of a situation. If the logical, business-like solution falls on deaf ears, and you really must react, you will need a plan B.

My suggestion for a plan B has two parts. First, when planning your workload for the year ahead, you need to plan for a certain number of "rush" projects that may crop up suddenly. You will need to leave a little breathing room in your scheduling calendar for these projects. The second part of plan B is to choose your staple contract graphic designers carefully. Know their particular skills, strengths, and weaknesses as best you can. You may either want to bring a contractor in to execute the rush project, or bring a contractor in to take over some work on an existing project, thus freeing some time for one of your in-house graphic design staff.

It is critical that you track, and document, these sudden, out-of-the-blue, rush projects very carefully. When did they appear? Who in the company requested this rush project? How often does this individual or group make such requests? How much additional money does a rush project typically cost? Is this more expensive than factoring such a project into the normal, scheduled workload for your group? This kind of precise documentation will help you enormously in the future.

All design managers should proactively write a year-end department report whether you are required to create such a report or not. This report should be sent to your immediate manager first. If he or she would be in agreement with the contents of your year-end report, identify other executives who should get a copy of the report. Other executives might include: Finance, Procurement, and Internal Audit, among possible other departments.

Among many topics covered in the report, the effects of unplanned rush projects on both budget and staff must be documented. By documented, I mean verifiable factual information. Unless you call attention to all the facets of your work, no one will ever think you have any difficulties or opportunities for improvement. I am convinced executives or managers who come to you to satisfy their need for graphic design projects believe they are the only ones in the company with such needs. They also tend to believe their project must be your highest priority!

This all comes down to developing realistic criteria for prioritizing graphic design projects in your company. Once these criteria have been developed, you must get complete buy-in from the highest level of executive management you can find. Once approved, the criteria for prioritizing graphic design projects must be published and made available to every facet of the company. It has to become part of corporate policy.

The criteria for prioritizing graphic design projects must include benefit to the company, cost(s), and the metrics for determining these benefits and costs. These approved criteria for prioritization will make your scheduling much easier. You now have an approved corporate policy to refer to!

CHAPTER 11

Hiring and Terminating Employees

CONGRATULATIONS! THERE IS AN OPPORTUNITY for you to hire a new graphic designer to join your group. This may be because someone in your group has retired, moved on to another company, or perhaps you have received the green light to enlarge your staff. It may also be because you had the unfortunate task of terminating an existing employee. We will talk about termination later in this chapter.

The opportunity to hire someone must not be taken lightly. We are all aware that occasionally we make mistakes. Making a mistake in hiring someone for an in-house corporate design group could be extremely disastrous for your group's position as a strategic business partner, of being valued as a core competency, and to not only your group reputation in the company, but the design manager's credibility as well. Once you have hired the wrong person to join a corporate group it can be very difficult to terminate them and to manage them. In many cases, the burden of a bad hire can disrupt work flow, productivity, and group morale. It is critical to make good hires!

Hiring a graphic designer for your group should not be a casual effort on your part. Since you have now transitioned to a strategic partner role, rather than the traditional service provider group, you will want to look for professional graphic designers who can add value to your department.

There are many ways to find potential candidates for a job opening. You might choose to advertise the position either in print publications or online through LinkedIn or other services, engage the services of an employment agency, or work through professional design organizations such as AIGA, or DMI. You might even decide to utilize multiple sources.

No matter which method you decide to use the absolute first step is to carefully analyze the job opening and determine exact specs which will define the person you are looking for. This may be a great opportunity to find someone who can fill certain gaps you might have in skill sets, find someone with real experience working in a strategic thinking/partner relationship, or someone who can add genuine, noticeable value to your group. Of course there will be the evaluation of the person's design skills, but more than likely you will want someone who also has considerable business savvy. I also suggest in your planning for this position that you look out five or ten years. The design profession has changed rapidly over the last twenty years, and will most likely continue to evolve rapidly over the next ten or twenty years. Technology in design changes every few months these days, and a candidate's knowledge of current graphic design technology as well as planned enhancements will be a critical factor in your search.

Also take into consideration where your *company* is headed in the future. There are so many mergers, acquisitions, alliances, and R&D efforts going on in the corporate world today that you need to take all of that into consideration.

Perhaps a bit dramatic, but a good example anyway, would be Kodak. For what seems forever, Kodak was the biggest name in film. One would have thought that path would continue forever. However, that whole industry changed rapidly with a shift to digital photography. Now, rather than focusing on chemical film products and cameras, Kodak has had to make a major shift to embrace digital photography. But what is next? If you are working in an industry that is changing quickly, take that all into consideration when you are developing a profile for the kind of graphic designer you will need in the future.

You will also need to consult/partner with your HR experts. Does your company have any standards or guidelines for new hires? This might likely include diversity requirements for internal staffs. Those requirements are fine with me, but you need to know what they are. Some companies also have restrictions as to pay scales and re-location reimbursements. You need to be up-to-date on all these requirements before beginning your search for a new employee.

Once you have done your homework, thoroughly, you will need to write a job description. This job description should be reviewed by your HR partner before you take it public.

Once you (and the company) are satisfied with the job description you are ready to "post" the opening for the design community to see, and/or meet with a search agency who will conduct the search on your behalf. Also, do not forget about your personal network. People in your network might just know the type of person you are looking for.

Another scenario is that you might already know someone who would be ideal for the position. Keep in mind that person may already be happily working for someone else. If you are truly eager to recruit them, they will sense that, and they most likely will want to negotiate significant salary and benefits before they leave their current employer to join your group. Be prepared by knowing just what your upper limits are for salary, benefits, and other perks like office space. I once wanted to offer a very talented graphic designer a job in my group. He was very enthusiastic at first and we had several discussions. The salary and benefits were worked out to everyone's satisfaction. And then the bombshells dropped. He told me he would have to have a large, floor-to-ceiling walled office, with a door. The office had to be a corner office with large windows on two sides. He needed his own administrative assistant. He wanted the company to pay all of his cell phone expenses (including personal calls). Finally, he wanted a reserved parking spot in the corporate headquarters' parking garage! Of course, these demands became the deal breaker. He had all the qualities I was looking for, but the company wasn't about to provide all the special perks he said he needed in order to leave his current position.

Another thing to keep in mind is that you might be flooded with resumes very quickly. More than likely you will receive more resumes from people than you can possibly interview. As I write this chapter, the economy is still sluggish and there are a great many graphic designers looking for permanent employment in an in-house group. That may change in the future, but currently there is no shortage of candidates for in-house graphic design positions. Because of this, it is even more important that you prepare a very detailed job description. If you can, enlist some help in reviewing all these resumes. Have a detailed checklist handy. Unless a potential candidate seems to meet at least 80% of the items on your checklist, stop consideration of this person. Also, set a deadline for submission of resumes. Otherwise they will continue to come into your office for months and months.

Have the courtesy to acknowledge receipt of every resume. Don't say, "Thanks, but no thanks" just yet. Simply tell everyone that all resumes are being reviewed and evaluated and that you will get back to them once the deadline for submission has passed.

After this initial screening process, you may still find there are more candidates than you can possibly interview. So a second review of "semi-finalists" will be necessary to whittle down the list. A third pass may also be required. Your goal should be to identify the top twelve candidates (the finalists).

You will now need to contact each of these people and invite them to come in for an interview. I also find it expedient to ask them to send their portfolio for your review prior to the interview. Most often, this can be done electronically through the Internet. Having a chance to review a portfolio prior to the formal interview will help you structure each applicant's interview session.

Set a firm date and time for each of these interviews. More than likely you will only be able to do two or possibly three in any one day. I would advise not trying to interview more than three people in a day. You have other work obligations, and you need the time to thoughtfully consider what each interviewee has told and shown you. If you try to cram too many interviews into a day, at the end of the day you may have difficulty recalling each of the candidates.

I am aware that some candidates for jobs these days request reimbursement for travel expenses to attend an interview. Check with your HR partner on this. If your company is willing to do this, fine. But most companies today will not offer such reimbursement. If there are extenuating circumstances, once again, consult with your HR partner.

Structuring the Interview

First, some general guidelines for the interviewing process as a whole. You should always interview at least four or five candidates for any job opening. You should not have any problem with this! You need to interview several candidates so you have a realistic basis for comparison. The ideal would be to have at least one, or two, other people interview each candidate. This could be someone from your group, or your HR partner. Never hire "on the spot." Allow a few days to elapse before you make any final decisions.

Always check references. Write down the questions you want to ask the candidate's references. Some suggestions might include, "How does he or she handle multiple projects all going on at once?" "What are some examples of how he or she added genuine value to a project?" "What was the greatest contribution he or she made to your organization?" I'm sure you will also think of other similar questions to ask.

Now, you must think about what questions you will ask in the actual interview with the candidate, beyond simply looking at his or her portfolio. Remember, it will be important to ask each candidate the same questions so you will have a strong basis for comparison.

The following are some of the questions I traditionally asked:

- If you come to work here, what would you expect to accomplish over the next five years?
- Take me through a typical day at your current employer.
- If applicable, why did you leave your last job?
- Give me a list of adjectives that best describe you.
- What was the greatest lesson you learned in your last job?
- How well do you interact with non-designers you need to work with?
- What is the worst thing going on in corporations today? Why?
- Do you have any personal goals in life as a professional graphic designer? What are they?

- Have you actively participated in any personal professional development programs? What were they?
- What was your greatest accomplishment as a graphic designer so far?
- Do you tend to work well alone on graphic design projects? Why, or why not?
- Who was your greatest mentor in your career as a graphic designer? Why was this individual so significant to your career?
- Where do you see yourself in five years if you join this graphic design group?
- Do you see yourself staying here until you retire?
- Why should I hire you?

These are just a few examples, I'm sure you will be able to come up with your own list.

Portfolio Review

For a graphic design position, a portfolio review is mandatory. You must see examples of the candidate's graphic design technique, style, and skill. As mentioned earlier, it is really very helpful if you can review the portfolio prior to the face-to-face interview. This will give you the chance to really study the samples in the portfolio, and to formulate some discussion points around the portfolio.

Ask the candidate several questions about each, or at least many, of the examples in the portfolio. This questioning will help you understand how the designer presents his or her work. Do they focus on "how they did it" (design technique), or how the design solution solved a real world problem? Do they demonstrate the ability to communicate design solutions strategically? Can they explain why the design solution was successful in the marketplace? Does the portfolio suggest the ability to work in different styles? I am sure you will be able to come up with the right questions. Do be careful. I have been quite disturbed to read blogs on the Internet that indicate too many graphic designers are including examples in their portfolio that either are not their work at all, or are samples of someone else's work that they simply had done some final production work on.

It only happened to me once, but a candidate included a very nice logo in his portfolio that I had designed six years earlier!

Once you have identified one or two likely candidates, it is prudent to interview each of them a second time. During this second interview, probe deeper into their personal philosophy of graphic design and their methods of approaching a graphic design project. Try to ascertain how well they would fit into your group and how well they would work with their colleagues. Finally, if you have had someone else interview the candidate as well, discuss each of your evaluations candidly. Don't try to make the final decision by yourself.

Terminating an Employee

There is probably no worse part of your job as manager of the group than the need to terminate an employee. If the individual has been caught stealing, using narcotics in the workplace, or some similar infraction, the task is somewhat easier. However, this is rarely the reason you feel you need to terminate the employee. Usually it is for extremely sub-standard performance.

In today's corporate environment, nearly all companies have very strict guidelines to follow before you can actually fire someone. Once again, consult with your HR partner, describe the situation as fairly and accurately as possible, then review all corporate guidelines which relate to the situation. Most companies require a rather lengthy process of meetings with the employee to discuss poor performance issues, offering help to the employee in correcting these performance issues, and realistic goal setting on a month by month basis. Frankly, the whole process could take a year or more. The employee needs to have time to correct the performance issues with your help.

During this process is critical to document every meeting with the employee, every goal that is set for him or her, and to document every way in which you have tried to help the employee. Your HR partner's involvement in all of this is a standard requirement.

You must be totally honest at all times with the employee. You need to be very specific about all the issues that have brought you both to this point.

Managing Sub-Standard Performance Problems

There seems to be two prevalent techniques I have noted during my career as a consultant. On the one hand, there are design managers who tend to overwhelm and intimidate an employee who has demonstrated poor performance. And then there are the design managers who are very non-confrontational. They actually fear dealing with the issue, hoping the employee will "get up to speed" by themselves. Neither of these scenarios will ultimately work very well. The performance problems will not just go away without some type of managerial intervention. A frank discussion between manager and employee must happen sooner than later.

The design manager's primary objective is to plan and manage the discussion in a way which will be helpful to both the manager and the employee. Focusing on this objective up front will help you, the design manager, set a style and tone for the meeting. It should be open and participative. The key is to position the discussion as a problem solving opportunity. This means the design manager must clearly state the nature of the performance problem and have specific measurable data to document the problem. This should be done in a nonthreatening manner. The meeting will not go well if your employee feels immediately threatened.

Once the problem area(s) are on the table, it will be necessary for the design manager and the employee to explore, collaboratively, various ways to address the issues. Your goal in this first meeting is to list a number of possible solutions, as well as opportunities, for improving the employee's overall performance. Be sure to write down each acceptable idea. If your employee suggests something that is just not going to be an acceptable solution, carefully explain to him or her why the suggestion will not work. The employee's commitment to the solutions you agree on will be much greater if those solutions come from him or her, rather than you. Avoid the mistake of trying to solve the problem yourself. Presenting an employee a list of ultimatums will most likely be met with resistance and later accusations by the employee that you did not give them a chance to discuss various goals and objectives. It is most desirable if a potential goal or solution requires some effort on your part as design manager, as well as on your employee's part.

Agree on milestones, or specific dates for specific improvements. You must use valid criteria for these goals and improvements. This will underline the immediate importance of resolving issues satisfactorily. If your employee hasn't achieved specific goals in the agreed time frame, clearly discuss what further actions might be necessary. Absolute clarity during such a meeting is mandatory.

If ultimate termination of employment is a possibility if the employee doesn't meet the agreed to goals for improvement, you must be sure of the following:

- The data used to make a termination decision must be measurable. It is not possible to really measure things like attitude, aggressiveness, and emotional feelings. If you are approaching termination, the reasons for this action need to be objective and highly measurable.
- Consistency. All employees have to be measured by the same criteria.
- Discrimination. All employees—men, women, minorities, different ethnicities and ages, etc.—must be treated the same way.
- All decisions for termination must be strictly job related.

If, unfortunately, an employee's employment must be terminated for documented poor performance, and lack of ability to improve performance, then it will be necessary for the manager to have extensive data and documentation for the decision. You, the design manager, cannot rely on vaguely remembering you talked to the employee once about improving their performance! Put everything in writing, including when, where, what, and measurable data based on the results of an employee's work. Be sure all documentation is objective and measurable. You cannot say simply, "This employee is lazy and uncooperative at times." That becomes your personal, un-measurable opinion. Always document sub-standard performance right away, it is not wise to try to remember problems that might have arisen some time ago.

A Better Alternative to Termination

I don't think I have ever met a design manager who actually enjoys the thought of terminating one of his or her graphic designers. An alternative to reaching this point would be to frankly discuss with the employee in the first sub-standard performance meeting the possibilities of the employee finding suitable employment on their own elsewhere. I recall one such discussion with one of my graphic designers. At our first meeting I carefully explained the issues with his performance. The issues did not revolve around his skills or talent as a graphic designer, but rather the issues revolved around not getting projects done on time, not doing the best design work I knew he was capable of, not being truly collaborative with other designers in the group, and numerous complaints from our non-design business partners about his apparent lack of interest in their projects.

As we openly talked in this meeting, it became clear that this designer simply deplored working in an in-house graphic design group. He didn't accept the culture of a corporation, and he felt trapped in a job he really didn't enjoy. We then discussed various solutions, including that he might feel more motivated in an agency setting. He agreed that option appealed to him far more than being part of an in-house corporate design group. We did also discuss ways in which he could improve his performance as part of our in-house group, and set some specific milestone dates to make these improvements. But he also told me he would begin immediately looking for a job with an agency.

His performance did show improvement in our in-house group, but I am sure it was because he saw a better future for himself in an agency setting. Within just three months he told me had been offered a position with a well-known agency and had accepted the offer. He gave me one month's notice of his resignation date.

This alternative solution worked for the best for everyone. He was not fired. I have kept in touch with him over the years and he has thanked me many times for making him realize a career with an independent agency was best for him. He thrived in his new position! I was very happy for him, and he was very happy to be out of the corporate world, which he really wasn't suited for in the first place. It became a happy ending.

CHAPTER 12

The Annual Performance Review

In Chapter 10 we discussed the issue of working with an employee who was experiencing noticeable sub-standard performance. We will shift gears in this chapter to focus on the annual performance review. Just about every corporation I know requires this annual performance review for *all* employees.

These annual employee performance reviews are deemed necessary by corporations to maintain uniformity in decisions around salary and for planning for legitimate staffing levels. However, there are other purposes. While the more formal review is used primarily for classification reasons by the company, the more informal value of these annual reviews is to benefit both the manager and the employee. If done properly the employee should become more motivated and thus more productive. The employee will also find greater clarity around the manager's expectations for the group as well as for themselves. Hopefully, the employee will also leave the session feeling a greater sense of responsibility and support from the manager.

The manager has an opportunity to spend some time every year evaluating each individual employee and reviewing current and immediate future needs for specific skill sets for the group. By setting aside some time to focus on each single employee, the manager will be able to better assess not only each employee's strengths and opportunities for improvement, but also to take an objective look at the design team as a whole.

It also provides both the manager and employee the opportunity to meet one-on-one at least once a year. In today's overloaded in-house graphic design groups, such one-on-one opportunities to meet have become vary rare. The workloads are so heavy that time just doesn't seem to exist for this kind of personal interaction. In the ideal world, such personal meetings would be far more frequent than once a year. But our worlds are not ideal, so a once-per-year meeting seems to be the only reasonable alternative.

The basic objectives of these annual reviews include:

- Clarity about what each employee needs to accomplish in the coming year, and how to do it.
- A frank evaluation of the employee's current quantity and quality of work.
- Setting some specific goals for the employee for the coming year.
- Setting time frames for meeting these goals.
- Agreeing to measurement metrics for each goal. (We will know when this particular goal has been met when the following XYZ is evident.)

Another objective of this annual review session is to be sure each employee feels supported, valued, and empowered. The goals need to be realistic, but not negotiated. It is the design manager's job to establish goals for the employee that will make him or her more valuable to the group. It is usually ideal to force the employee to "stretch" a bit more than they have in the past, or might do on their own. We need to help employees grow in their careers, and not just be happy with the status quo. The function of these reviews is to create a climate which inspires the employee's need to achieve and become more valued.

A Few Guidelines

Always notify an employee at least two weeks in advance that their performance review is scheduled for such-and-such a date and time. It is never appropriate to say, "Harry, come in to my office, I need to give you your annual performance review." The employee needs the time to prepare for this review as well as you do.

Prior to the annual review meeting with an employee, the design manager needs to do his or her homework. First, review copies of the previous year's annual performance review and the results of goal milestone meetings for the previous year. Honestly analyze the employee's overall development, progress, productivity, quality, and quantity of work for the preceding year. Develop realistic goals for each employee to meet in the coming year. Write out your evaluation of each employee. List professional development opportunities you would like to offer each employee.

If salary is increased, or kept the same at the time of each annual performance review in your company, be prepared to discuss the salary issue with the employee. If there is to be no increase in salary, be prepared to explain why this is the case. In short, be thoroughly prepared. Never try to "wing" it or you will telegraph to the employee a message of, "You are really not important enough for me to have spent much time on this before you came in."

Get out from behind your desk and sit next to your employee. Sitting behind your desk or across from the employee at a table signals an adversary relationship and implies negotiation is coming up. I am quite aware that nearly all managers' offices, in the United States, anyway, include not only the manager's desk, but also a small round table for discussions. This is fine in most situations; however, this type of personal performance review is best if done without a barrier between reviewer and reviewee, so try to sit next the employee being reviewed, not across the table from him or her. As I mentioned a performance review is not a negotiation. It is an honest and fair analysis of personal performance, coupled with setting some goals that the design manager has developed for the employee's ultimate benefit.

Go over with each employee's last year's goals. Never say, "You didn't do very well." That will set a negative reaction to everything which will follow. It would be better to simply say "some of the goals we set last year were not met." If goals were not achieved, ask questions such as, did we overestimate? What occurred that we didn't anticipate or plan for? How can we do a better job this year? These questions cannot be judgmental. Seek factual information, not a string of excuses.

Ask the employee questions such as: "Were you as productive as you should have been?" "What unforeseen obstacles arose to meeting your goals?" "Is there something I could have done to help you more?" "If so, why didn't you come to me for help?"

The annual review must be focused on the future. We learn from the past, but we plan for the future. The desire should be to set challenging, realistic goals for the future. Working together, the manager and employee agree on the what, how, and when of each future goal. This should result in the employee and manager both ending the session feeling it was a win-win meeting.

CHAPTER 13

Presenting Design Solutions for Approval

It has always been fascinating to me that in the corporate world the people with the final approval responsibility for graphic design projects are always non-designers with no real knowledge of graphic design. This has come about mostly because, as I mentioned earlier, they are business people with a strong knowledge of the business problem to be solved. They really do not believe designers have the same understanding of the business need for a graphic design solution; therefore, they need to make the final decision about the appropriateness of the design solution.

This whole business of gaining approval for a graphic design solution is among the most painful and frustrating processes in-house graphic design groups face on a routine basis. I certainly suffered through these approval meetings for a number of years early in my career as an in-house corporate design manager. Finally, I had to face the fact that I needed to find a way to take the pain, frustration, and suffering away. At first, I thought it might be a hopeless quest—the impossible dream, if you will.

I recalled that in design school, I had one graphic design professor who, at the time, I thought was particularly harsh with this approval process. Finally I realized that, in fact, he wasn't harsh at all—he was just preparing us for our careers!

He would assign a graphic design problem for us to work through. On the appointed day when our solutions were to be presented, he would have us put our work along the ledge of the whiteboard in the classroom. Without saying a word, he would walk along the board and either leave your work where it was, or throw it on the floor! Actually, almost everybody's work ended up on the floor. He would then turn to the class and say, "Everything on the floor fails. If you think your work hasn't failed, pick it up, put it back up on the ledge, and tell me and the class why it doesn't fail." Of course, most of us picked up our work and tried to defend it. After all, we didn't want to fail. While we desperately tried to defend our work, the professor kept interrupting by saying; "You're too proud and defensive of your clever design solution, put it back on the floor!"

What he was teaching us is that design should not be defended. Design should not be a success because *we* thought so. Rather, we only got to keep our work up on the ledge when we could clearly explain why our solution met the objectives of the assignment. For some reason, it took me a few years to really understand what this professor had taught us. It was always too easy in school to talk a lot about how clever (creative, etc.) we had been with an assignment. Other design students knew what we were talking about, and were often very supportive. This is not the case in the corporate world. The other non-design-trained stakeholders, particularly those who have the authority to approve—or disapprove—a design solution, are not cognizant of all the design techniques we know. They only know whether they "like it" or not.

The particular professor I am referring to was actually quite unique in his approach. What he was doing is certainly not the norm in most graphic design classrooms today.

I have had the privilege of attending and speaking at a few *HOW Magazine* design conferences. At the HOW conferences, one evening is devoted to an event called "The Student Showcase." The conference organizers invite graphic design school students who are in their final year of study to bring their portfolios and display their work for all of the conference attendees. I really look forward to this annual event. I am often amazed at the talent, creativity, and ability displayed by these students.

I attended one of these Student Showcase events and spotted one student whose work was particularly impressive. The young man was a graphic design student and had a large display of posters and brochures he had designed. As I approached the table where he was presenting his portfolio, I overheard him explaining one of his brochures to an attendee of the conference. With a great deal of excitement and intensity, the young man explained that on the first spread he had introduced an emotional experience. On the next spread, he had enhanced this experience by adding bold colors and avant-garde typographic treatments. Finally, he explained, he combined all of these design elements to bring the brochure to an exciting, emotional climax!

What this student was doing was explaining the design techniques he had considered and used to create what he believed to be a visually stunning piece. To another designer, his work was indeed visually stunning. However, if he had used that kind of thinking in making a presentation of a brochure to a non-design-trained CEO or marketing vice president, he would have been in big trouble.

Let me assure you, I am not trying to belittle this student. He was doing what he was used to doing in design school. In design school, we present our work to fellow graphic design students and graphic design teachers. It seems normal to present graphic design, well, as design. Unfortunately, this doesn't work in the corporate world. The people we will present graphic design solutions to in the business world don't understand—or appreciate—the power of using negative space, bold color palettes, or unique typographic styles brilliantly. After we leave design school, we have to learn to present design solutions for final approval by non-design business managers in an entirely new way.

The key is not to try to *defend* design solutions by talking about design elements, but to present the *results* of the design solution vis-à-vis the business objectives of the project. It is up to us, the graphic designers, to point out why a particular design solution works to meet the stated business objectives. We take it away from the subjective and move it into the objective. The objective is found in the design brief, which then also becomes your approval presentation outline.

The Design Brief as an Outline for Approval Presentations

If you have carefully constructed a design brief as outlined earlier, then you have effectively created an outline for your approval presentation as well. I am talking about approval of a final graphic design solution at this point, not various and sundry preliminary approvals throughout the course of the project.

Your presentation must begin with the very first paragraphs or bullet points in your design brief: the executive summary. You briefly review the key business elements: why we are doing this project (business objectives), why we are doing it now, whom we are doing it for, what business outcomes we expect, and so on. This sets up the facts that: (1) you thoroughly understand the project as well as the business objectives clearly, (2) you understand the target audience(s), and (3) you worked strategically, in a highly businesslike manner.

Next, I would suggest moving straight through the brief as you constructed it, mentioning briefly who is ultimately accountable for the results (the co-owners) and who the key stakeholders are, and giving an overview of the various phases of the project. This should be followed by a description of the particular industry category (or categories) and current industry trends, the company portfolio (if applicable), certainly the target audience, and any other key elements that you may have included in your particular brief.

When you get to the detail of the design phases, be sure to clearly explain, in layman's terms, the content of the phase, why it was critical, who was involved, what, if any, approvals were made in the phase and by whom, and the results of any target audience testing that may have been done. The purpose of all of this is to make certain the approver understands there was a strategic, businesslike process followed, and that key stakeholders were involved. The results of testing with target audience(s) demonstrate that your solution is not just the "decorative whim" of some artist!

Target Audience Testing

I have become a dedicated believer in target audience testing of graphic design solutions at various points in the design process for major, highly strategic graphic design projects. This needn't be either expensive or overly time consuming. Rather, it will give you an opportunity to determine if you are on the right track or not.

The best way I have found to do this testing is to partner with the sales force. More than likely your graphic design solution will be used by sales people, making sales calls on the actual members of your target audiences. Sales people love to participate in this way. I recall one sales manager who told me this involvement with the sales force by graphic design had previously been unheard of in the company. He was more than ready, willing, and able to partner with us!

We are designing something for a target audience, more than likely several target audiences. Who better to inform us whether we are succeeding or not than the people we are designing for?

I have often been told by non-design business managers that external testing of graphic design is absolutely not necessary. After all, there are plenty of people right in the corporate offices that can tell you whether your design concepts are appropriate or not. This is completely untrue!

Permit me to make an analogy. Mom and dad have a newborn baby. Mom and dad and all the relatives believe this is the most beautiful baby that ever arrived on this planet. However, the neighbors down the street think this baby is really unattractive. The moral is that the immediate family is not capable of making a truly unprejudiced judgment. The immediate family is too close to the event to be completely objective.

In a way, all those good people in the corporate headquarters are just like the immediate family. They are too involved, too close to the situation to make an objective decision. As graphic designers we must have objective, outside opinions of our concepts and design solutions. The place to find these truthful, objective opinions is outside of the company, namely from the target audiences. Internal people will be too biased.

At the point at which we had three or more possible conceptual design directions, I would call a local sales office and ask if one of our designers could spend a day accompanying a sales person on actual sales calls. I let the sales people know we needed only a few minutes with the customer at the sales call and would not interfere in any way with the sales call itself. Please remember, I didn't do this for every single graphic design project, only the highly strategic, critical, major projects.

My designers would take about five minutes at the end of the sales call with the customer. He or she would show the customer the three or four concept sketches we were considering. The simple questions for the customer were: What message does each of these concepts convey to you? Which of these concepts appeals most to you? Why? Are any of these concepts believable to you? Note we never let ourselves jump into the subjective arena by asking, "Which of these do you *like?*"

Sometimes, the concept most favored by my graphic design group was not the first choice of customers! We might have only done this exercise with eight or so customers, but the exercise gave us incredible insight as to which of our conceptual directions were working best to meet the business objectives of a major graphic design project. At times we even realized that none of our initial concepts were working quite as well as we had hoped.

This rather simple, unscientific concept testing saved us a great deal of time. We were no longer guessing; we were getting rather simple initial feedback from actual members of the target audience we were designing for.

After this initial foray into target audience land, we were able to refine our concept(s) based upon actual target audience feedback.

Later, we would take out more polished concepts and repeat the process with different members of the target audience. Once again, the purpose was to be certain we were on the right track with our design solution. We would also seek the feedback of salespeople; after all, they were the people who would be using our material to make a sale.

Once we had the final solution (hopefully!) we would take just that concept out to the target audience one last time. This time our questions would be more specific: "What message does this piece convey to you?": Would this piece motivate you to learn more about this project?" "After seeing this piece, would you want to buy this product?" There could be other questions too, depending on the business purpose(s) of the piece, but you get the idea.

Understanding the Final Approver

People who have the authority and power to make final approvals of graphic design solutions are human beings. Human beings all have unique personalities (refer back to Chapter 8). Therefore, it behooves you and your co-owner/business partner to find out as much as you can about the individual you will be presenting to. What motivates him or her? What basic needs does he or she have that frame his or her personality? Is he or she primarily motivated by power? Does he or she need to be clearly in control of everything, all of the time? If so, perhaps you need to keep this in mind as you prepare your presentation.

Other senior managers I have known are really more motivated by achievement. They are very proud of the things they have been able to accomplish in their careers. And they are usually very proud of the success their business has achieved so far. More than likely I would use a different style of presentation content for this type of individual. I would probably want to include something about how this represents yet another achievement for the company.

Finally, a common type of personality I have run into in the ranks of very senior management is the people who are really driven by the need for affiliation. Down deep, they want to be connected with everyone—customers, employees, and shareholders. My style of presentation would be geared to this need differently than one I would prepare for a power person or an achievement-driven manager. I would mention at the very least, "When we tested this solution with real customers, they were delighted!"

It is never enough to just create a one-size-fits-all presentation for approval of a design solution. Keep the audience for your presentation clearly in mind as you prepare for an approval meeting. It will help ensure a successful outcome to the meeting.

It is important to remember that very often the person (or persons) with final approval authority have not given this project one single thought until this very meeting. Usually they have not been involved throughout the design process, and therefore they need to be reminded, or told for the first time, what this project is all about in business terms. Do not talk about design! Talk about the *results* of the design project, and how those results meet the business objectives. It is not necessary to rave on about your creative use of typography, color palettes, or other design elements. It is not necessary to invite subjective criticism. *Never* ask, "Do you like it?" (Invariably they won't!)

Subjective Comments Versus Objective Discussion

Is graphic design subjective? Of course it is. However, it is also a problem-solving discipline and that fact allows us to move discussions about graphic design into the realm of objectivity. If we allow subjective comments to dominate any conversations about the results of graphic design, we are asking for trouble.

Personal opinions must be taken off the table when discussing graphic design solutions, especially when you are seeking approval for a design solution from non-design trained executives.

If I were an artist, and painted your portrait, you are entitled to look at the finished painting and say, "I don't like it." Fine, that is your personal opinion. It is okay to express personal opinions when talking about fine art. I actually know people who have said they "don't like" the Mona Lisa. They are telling the truth. They personally don't like that painting.

I might say, "I really like blue," and you might say, "I like red." Two honest, intelligent people have just told each other what they personally like or dislike. Where does the discussion go from here? Nowhere, there can be no further discussion about our personal likes and dislikes. I personally like blue, end of story.

Graphic design on the other hand is not about personal likes and dislikes. Graphic design solutions are about what works or does not work to solve a well-defined problem, or meet a specific business objective. We cannot allow personal feelings to enter into the discussion.

When I was in the corporate world, one particular senior executive really impressed me with his feelings about this subject. When he called a meeting he would tell the attendees that no personal opinions could be expressed in his meeting. No one could say, "I like," I don't like," "I believe," "I think," "It is my opinion," or any other comment which indicated a personal opinion. His direction to the group was that this was a meeting about business, and not about how each attendee personally felt about some issue. He would further explain there was not enough time to engage in such trivia. He asked them to leave their personal opinions outside of his meetings. He wanted the discussions to be about what works, and what doesn't work, and why. He was all business. I admired that in a corporate setting. I had attended endless meetings in the past that went nowhere. A topic was put on the table, people expressed their opinions and no decisions were made except to schedule the next meeting on the particular topic. A complete waste of time!

So how do you handle the inevitable subjective comments in a graphic design solution approval meeting? How do you respond when the approver says, "I don't like it?" The trick is to move from the subjective comment to an *objective* discussion. I would acknowledge the subjective comment by saying, "That is very critical to me. Why don't you like it? What is it about this solution that is not working to solve the identified problem?" This technique allows you to move from subjective comment, to objective discussion. Oftentimes, the person making the comment will reply, "I don't know, I just don't like it." This is your opportunity to go back to the testing results you gathered from the target audience. Tests with our customers prove that they got the message, wanted to buy, or whatever the objective might be. You must be sure to keep objectivity in the forefront and not allow personal subjective opinions to remain on the table.

How Many Graphic Design Solutions Do You Present for Approval?

It is very dangerous to present more than one graphic design solution in a *final* approval meeting—even if there are two or three solutions you know might also work. If you present multiple design solutions, I can almost guarantee the approver will tell you that he or she "likes" certain elements of each solution you present and will ask, "Could you combine those various elements into one design?" What you will end up with is a hybrid solution that doesn't work. This approval process must not turn into a beauty contest. Design is a problem-solving discipline. Focus on the problem, and on how the single graphic design solution you are presenting solves that business problem. Also, if you indicate there are two or three solutions that might work, you are simply signaling to the approver that you are not really sure which solution is the best. You are relinquishing ultimate accountability.

But what if, as many designers tell me is the case, the approver always insists that he or she wants to see at least two or three solutions? Ask yourself, Why is this the case? They want to see multiple solutions because they don't *trust you* to come up with a single business-oriented solution on your own. They don't believe you know as much about their business need(s) as they do. They agree you can do design well, but they are the ones who will decide which design solution works best to solve the problem. This situation exists primarily because you have probably always presented graphic design solutions in design terms, not business terms. They are not used to hearing you talk about meeting business objectives.

To turn this situation around, you will initially have to be very careful in developing your presentation, and to be sure to mention the many concepts you explored—and *tested*—with the target audience. You should also be sure to mention that throughout the project, key stakeholders were actively involved, and that these stakeholders had agreed to the end result of each phase. This indicates to the final approver that there were, in fact, multiple treatments considered, but this single one was the solution that best met the business criteria and objectives. If they still want to see other treatments, then simply say you will be back in a week or so to show them what had been considered, and explain why each of these early concepts had been rejected by the target audience during testing, the graphic design team and by the key stakeholders. This is particularly effective since you have tested concepts with the target audience(s), and can indicate that your target business audience(s) preferred the design solution you are presenting. In time, approvers will—hopefully—trust you more, and be satisfied that you will only bring them graphic design solutions for approval that really work in the marketplace to the benefit of the company.

If you absolutely must talk about certain design elements, don't do it until *after* you have made the business case for your design solution. Too many designers begin these approval presentations with lots of comments about specific design elements. This opens the door for the approver to jump in with highly personal and *subjective* comments. Always make the *objective* business case first.

Another critical aspect of creating an approval presentation is to be sure to include the last two phases of any graphic design project: implementation and measurement. By including these in your approval presentation, you will demonstrate your acceptance of accountability for the outcome(s) of the particular project. The approver will appreciate knowing a bit of detail about what will happen as the result of his or her approval, and will definitely respond well to the fact that there are specific business criteria in place to measure results in business terms.

Anticipating Objections

When you are preparing your approval presentation, think about your approver, and what objections he or she is likely to raise. In graphic print design, the two most common objections I encountered were: "Isn't the type awfully small?" and "Shouldn't the company logo be larger?" Clearly there are many others that you could add from your own experience! The point is to anticipate these kinds of comments, and to deal with them as you make your presentation in a way that will ensure the comments will never be made.

As an example, I remember presenting a design solution for a new corporate stationery system. This happened to be a very high priority for my CEO, and he was certainly one of those "Shouldn't the logo be larger, and the type be larger?" guys. A prime business objective of this project was to be sure that people in more than forty countries would all use the identical stationery system. Customers had been teasing the CEO about how his company "looked so different" in various parts of the world. He had taken this teasing very personally, and was determined to solve the problem. This CEO was very driven by the need for affiliation. He desperately needed to be loved and appreciated by everyone. He took these comments to mean, "We do not approve of you and your company." That is why this particular project was so critical to him. We understood this personality need of his, and therefore created a presentation that would ease his mind. We were careful to note that a solution had been found that would satisfy, and *delight,* customers worldwide.

In order to address his anticipated comments about type size and logo size, we created our final approval presentation for the single system we had developed, target audience tested, and were recommending, taking extra care to mention to the CEO that part of solving the problem was to accommodate often lengthy addresses, postal codes, telephone information, etc., worldwide. We also pointed out that one reason various countries had developed their own unique stationery systems was that the amount of information required either by law or by standard geographical business practice was quite different from the U.S. standard. Names and titles were often much longer. Some countries required business registration numbers to be included on all business papers. In most countries that used both their native language and English, both sides of the business card or calling card were used. Also, both languages might appear on the same page of a letterhead or other business form.

If the prime business objective was to create a single system that could be used globally, then that system had to be able to accommodate all of this diverse information as well as all of the various specific country needs. We went on to explain that the maximum amount of information, along with the standard sizes of business papers in each country, were used as two of many guidelines to determine the most workable and effective size of the type on the business papers, as well as the placement and size of the company logo. We also explained that our solution had been tested and deemed successful by representatives of the target audience in each geographical region.

Now, this may seem like a lot of extra effort in an approval presentation, but it accomplished our goal. How could the CEO say the type was too small, or the logo was too small, after we had carefully explained a process that had led us to a solution that ultimately met the prime business objective? We had anticipated some of his comments and objections and effectively dealt with them in our presentation. He never raised the issue. If he *had* still asked if the type couldn't be larger, we would have answered by reiterating our process, and focusing a bit more on how well the solution had been received by various country managers when we asked them to review it with their customers. I would never get into a debate over the size of the typeface or the use of a specific font in an approval presentation, particularly with a CEO. I know I would lose. The trick is to use rational, businesslike discourse in an approval presentation, to not dwell on the relative merits of some design element, and to anticipate possible negative, or subjective, comments from the approver. Again, explain why it *works,* not why it is pretty.

What If You Can't Make the Presentation Yourself?

In some companies, unfortunately, the graphic designer or graphic design manager has not traditionally been allowed to present his or her own design solutions to the final approver. Someone else decides that he or she will do it for you!

There are a number of ways to deal with this.

In the beginning, before you have reached that point where you have credibility and trust as a strategic graphic design manager, you might have to temporarily live with this obstacle. The best thing to do in these situations is to create the type of presentation I have been discussing anyway and give it to the individual who is scheduled to present for you. A couple of things could happen at this point. The person might simply say "Thank you," and go off and do the presentation alone. In this case, at least the person has a bulletproof set of materials to use. After all, you created the presentation! A better scenario would be for the person to say, "You really ought to come with me." And, of course, the very best result is that the person would say, "You do this so well, why don't you come with me, and make the presentation yourself?"

Over time, your ultimate goal is to always be the one who makes graphic design solution presentations for approval. The concept of having co-owners in developing the brief, who are equal partners and equally accountable, should also help you in making the argument that approval presentations must be made by those who are *accountable* at the end of the day. It takes time to change company cultures and traditions. Don't panic if you find it will be necessary to slowly migrate to a new tradition of graphic design solutions always being presented by graphic design professionals. The key is that you are moving forward, not simply accepting the status quo as a *fait accompli.*

What If You Are Just Not Comfortable Making Presentations to Senior Managers?

I know many talented designers and design managers who just cannot stand up in front of a group, or even a single senior manager, and make an effective presentation. For some of these people, a solution is to take some courses or get some coaching on effective public speaking. For others, it might be hopeless. They just aren't comfortable in these situations, and it shows. For this latter case, I would suggest enlisting the aid of your co-owner, non-design business partner to stand up and make the presentation. It doesn't mean you can't develop the presentation, it just means that it is important to present the design solution in the most effective, compelling way, and that might mean getting some help from your business partner. However, you still must be present at the presentation. To not show up would signal that you are really not accountable for your design solution.

A Final Word on Approvals

This may startle you, but a mentor of mine, early in my career, once said to me, "Never ask for approval, simply thank the approver for it!" I must admit, I was pretty skeptical about this approach at first. I had not yet reached the point where I was completely trusted and had the kind of credibility that would allow me to be so brash, especially in the presence of the CEO! At first I waffled a bit and said things to the CEO like, "I'm sure you will agree with us, and the target audience(s) that this is the best graphic design solution to meet our business objectives." I was equally startled to find out that this tactic actually worked! Once I reached that point, I never went back. I never again said, "We *hope* you will approve." Much later, I was actually able to say, "We appreciate your approval." My mentor told me, "When you ask for approval, or worse, *hope* for approval, you signal that the other person knows better than you do whether your graphic design solution actually works. If you know it works, stand up for it. Explain why it works in business terms that the approver can understand."

CHAPTER 14

Educating Non-Designers about the Graphic Design Process

AFTER MANY YEARS OF LECTURING, teaching, and consulting with in-house graphic design groups, I am convinced the graphic design profession has the highest "whine" factor in the world. "Why don't they respect me?" "Why don't they trust me?" "Why don't they value me?" "Why don't they give me enough time to properly do my work?" "Why don't they tell me what I need to know?" Why, Why, Why! It is constant whining!

It isn't "them"; it is "us" who are at fault. When my children were little, I often said to them, "Stop your whining!" Whining will get our profession nowhere. "They" don't get it, because "we" are not helping "them" to get it.

We have invested years of our lives studying and practicing the profession of graphic design. We understand this profession. It is not their fault that they do not have the same kind of knowledge and experience that we have. It is up to us, the graphic design profession, to educate our non-design business partners on our processes, needs, and methodologies. We must take the time to help them understand. No, we aren't going to teach them how to become designers. But we are going to inform them of our somewhat special needs and processes.

One of the best ways to do this is with the collaborative design brief development process I described briefly earlier in this book. Using the collaborative design brief development time to inform our business partners of our needs is totally non-threatening. After all, we aren't doing any graphic design work yet, we are simply describing a possible project, its objectives, and various requirements.

There is one part of the design brief process that is particularly good to use as an opportunity to educate our non-design partners about our needs. This is the section where we outline the various phases of the project.

Phases of the Design Process

This part of the design brief provides critical detail to the road map to success we are creating. It ensures that everyone involved has a clear understanding of, and is in agreement with, every aspect (phase) of the project. It can often lead to successful negotiations to get more time and budget for the project as well.

Creating this section provides the design team manager with the opportunity to break a design project down into its various discrete parts. By doing this, your partner begins to understand some of the detail involved in executing the project. Once we understand things better, we are usually able to appreciate them more!

Too often the design profession seems to keep its processes a carefully guarded secret. As a result, many non-design business people tend to think we just go in the back room, get creative, and come out with something that looks really good. That "artist" mentality again! By sitting with your partner and working through the project in phases, you will have the opportunity to educate your partner and to get acceptance for your time and budget requirements in order to complete the project successfully.

To accomplish this, the description of each phase must contain, at a minimum, the following items:

- Precise description of the phase (activity)
- Time frame for the phase
- People who will be involved in the phase (be sure to include key stakeholders such as IP lawyers, purchasing agents, market researchers, and so forth)
- Approvals of the particular phase (who, when, where, etc.)
- Budget for the phase

The number of phases will, of course, be determined by the specific project. The critical thing is to be sure the description of the phase is complete and understandable to everyone involved. The best way to proceed is to first create the ideal scenario *with* your partner.

Let's assume for this exercise that a key objective of this graphic design project is to gain competitive advantage in the marketplace. As an example, let's say the first phase of the proposed graphic design project involves completing a visual audit of the top three competitor's print materials.

Okay, this is a logical starting point. But now is the time to expand the discussion of this phase with your partner.

- Do we have an example or examples of all current artifacts in our company portfolio? If not, precisely who will gather this material? How long will that take?
- How about the competitors? Do we know who the three are?
- Do we have examples of their current materials or products for this audit? Who will provide these examples? How long will it take for them to provide these materials?
- Who will actually be involved in conducting the audit? What criteria should we apply to this audit?
- How will the results be presented? Who will they be presented to? How long will this part of the audit process take?
- What costs are involved to do this piece of the project? What are the start and end dates for this phase?
- Will this phase require any stakeholder involvement or approvals? If so, who will those people be?

I have often found that in this example of an audit process, my partner is blown away by the scope, effort, time, and expense that are involved. They are usually surprised that design concept work really shouldn't start until after the audit has been completed and the graphic design team has analyzed the results.

When you complete a similar analysis for each additional phase of the project with your partner and add up the costs, as well as time requirements, the total will likely show that more time and money are required than originally planned. Your business partner will probably be trembling. This is the point where the graphic design project manager says, "Okay, let's go back to each phase and see where we can make some cuts." For each suggested cut, you must ask each other, "What are the *business risks* of eliminating, or not fully funding, this activity?" Notice that I am saying "business risks." If you simply say, "The graphic design team won't want to eliminate this step," then your partner can say, "It doesn't matter what the graphic design team wants!" But if there is a business-related risk that could potentially affect the project's business objectives, it will be more likely that your partner will agree the cut shouldn't be made. What usually happens during this process is that an agreement is reached to provide some more time for the project, redefine the project's objectives, provide more funding, or all of the above.

What is occurring is a businesslike discussion of what is really required to achieve a specific business goal. The graphic design process is educational for your partner because he or she is a participant. It is very hard to disagree with something you have helped to create in the first place! As you do more and more of these with various partners, each begin to have a greater appreciation for the needs of graphic designers and the graphic design process. Once again, we have a win-win scenario.

The Last Three Phases

Clearly, every project will have to face a final approval phase. The brief should include details about this phase. When will the approval meeting occur? Who will ultimately have final approval authority? Who will make the approval presentation? What is the budget for creating the approval presentation? Many times people forget that creating a presentation for approval has some costs related to it. This must be included in the overall project budget. These presentations also take considerable time just to create.

Just because a design solution is approved doesn't mean the co-owners and the graphic design team can walk away from it! Once approved, the design has to be implemented. This might involve a printing process. It certainly will involve some type of distribution process. After all, you have done this project for a target audience. How does it get to them? The implementation is as much a part of the design project as concept development and refinement and must be part of the complete design brief. This is a place where many of the stakeholders you identified in your preliminary meeting will come into play. Procurement (purchasing), print production, sales force, warehousing, distribution, etc., might all be critical components of implementing your project. Specific dates and budget figures must also be included in the implementation phase description.

Finally, the last phase should always be measurement metrics. How will anyone know this design solution, this design project, was successful? Remember, you and your co-owner/partner have accepted accountability for the success or failure of this project. What criteria will be applied to this measurement process, and how long will it take? Is there a cost involved in the measurement process?

There are many ways to measure results of a graphic design project. The key to determining just how to measure the results of graphic design is to go back to the project's business objectives.

You will recall that up-front we answered the questions of why we are doing this project, why we are doing it now, what the desired outcomes are, and what the business objectives are. The answers to these questions provide the basis for measuring results. If the desired outcomes and business objectives were achieved, the design project was successful!

CHAPTER 15

Nurturing Creativity

THE WORD "CREATIVE" IS OFTEN used in our profession. Too often, as I mentioned earlier in this book, the word is linked with service, as in "Creative Services Department." Many business people refer to graphic designers (and others) as "creatives."

Just what does the word "creative" mean? There seem to be a great many definitions floating around the Internet, but they all seem to refer to the ability to create something new and useful. Creative people are regarded as original thinkers, rule breakers, interpreters, innovators, and as people who do not follow established rules.

Whatever definition you choose, graphic designers do actually (or should anyway), fall into your definition of "creative" people. Creative graphic design is a very good thing. Creative people are people we should surround ourselves with in a corporate, in-house graphic design department. But creativity needs to be nurtured and supported constantly. There is no single, "right way" to nurture creativity.

Much has been written in the last few years about the "Creative Economy." Just Google "Creative Economy" and read all about it! Basically, it focuses on the growing need for corporations to adapt quickly, innovate, and meet entirely new needs of our rapidly changing marketplaces. To survive economically, businesses have to move forward in very creative/innovative ways. It is no longer prudent for a business to follow run-of-the-mill ideas. The most successful enterprises today are the ones who pursue, and embrace, fresh thinking. They are the corporations who are constantly looking for new and better ways to make money.

Consider just a few of the dramatic changes in commerce over the last few decades. Books were written, then printed on paper, bound and sold in a place called a bookstore. Bookstores are slowly going away, being replaced by electronic availability of the contents of a book. We no longer need to tote around a heavy, hard bound edition of a book. What does this mean to the publishing industry? How will they move forward creatively?

Chemical film has been replaced by digital imagery. It is now far easier to pay bills on line, than to write checks, put them in an envelope, apply postage, and mail them. If you don't believe this is a major issue, read about the current financial dilemma the United States Postal Service is facing. Email has largely replaced writing letters by hand. In fact cursive writing is now not usually taught in our schools. Students learn keyboarding techniques instead. In my area we are seeing many new schools being built. They are all equipped with state-of-the-art technology. School libraries are full of computers—and yeah, they still have real books too.

I once worked for the second largest computer manufacturer in the world, Digital Equipment Corporation. The company no longer exists largely because it failed to embrace the creative concept of personal computing. The list could go on forever. We certainly do now live in an economy driven by creativity. Corporations need extensive creative thinking in all areas of endeavor. Unfortunately, many companies recognize this new need but still do not provide the climate or environment necessary to foster creativity.

This kind of creative thinking needs to exist in every department of the company. Since this book is directed toward in-house graphic design groups, I will deal with just that faction of the corporation.

Creative Graphic Designers

Actually, psychologists tell us everyone is creative. But this isn't enough, that innate creative flair has to be nurtured, trained, and allowed to manifest itself. Graphic designers are usually people who are passionate about letting their innate creativity be expressed through their work. In some venues, such as large design agencies, it seems a bit easier to nurture creativity. However, within the often-staid corporate culture and climate, graphic designers face an uphill battle trying to allow their creativity to flourish. Corporations still tend to value conformity highly. Creative people do not respond well to conformity and rules. Often corporations will describe to employees what can, and what cannot, be done. Creative people have a hard time accepting, "what can't be done." Creative people don't say, "It can't be done." Rather, they look for new ways in which it "can be done."

Physical Space for Graphic Design Work

Over the years I managed in-house graphic design groups, it was not at all unusual that my very best strategic graphic designers tended to do a great deal of design work at home. During the day in the office, they were required to attend many meetings with their business partners. When they finally had time to return to their cubicles, the corporate space was too small, very bland, and way too structured according to corporate standards for office space. After putting in a full day "at the office," they would return to their homes and do most of their best creative work there. Many put in regular late nights of design work. They were more creative at home, because the environment they created in their home was far more conducive to creative thinking.

This was not the healthiest way to work. Many times these highly creative strategic designers would arrive at the office just a little late in the morning, very tired, but bringing with them from home some of their best and most creative graphic design solutions. All this was necessary, because corporations, even today, rarely offer the type of physical environment in which a highly creative strategic graphic designer can function at their best. They are more nurtured creatively outside of the office.

In a corporate environment, it is essential for the graphic design manger to constantly lobby to create an environment which will allow graphic designers to explore experiment, think, try new things, and, yes, to fail occasionally. This environment needs a relaxed, central space where designers will feel safe. As I mentioned earlier, most corporations I have visited do not provide this type of environment (space) for graphic design. Rather, the graphic design group has pretty much the exact type of physical space that everyone else in the company has. Again, it is that love of conformity that corporations seem to have. I know I suffered under similar circumstances for many years as a graphic design manager. Finally, I learned that two of my mutually valuable relationships could help me a great deal.

The first were my friends in plant facilities. They were always the first to know of some floor space that could become available in the near future. I would partner with them to help me find the best space possible for the graphic design group.

I really got lucky when I was with the Gillette Company. Another product division was being moved from Chicago to the Boston headquarters. Plant facilities had to find contiguous space for roughly one hundred people. The best option was to relocate some existing groups, including graphic design, to another location in the building. *Carpe diem*, I seized the day! I met with my partner in plant facilities and asked to see all the possible spaces we would be moved to. Of course, they all looked exactly alike. Now the building we were in was a twenty-five story building. At the time, the Gillette Company occupied floors four through twenty-five. However, they did also have some space at the lobby level of the building which had formally been used for meetings. Basically, it was a small group of conference rooms. It was no longer being used very much for that purpose. I wanted the space for my group!

I then went to my partner in Human Resources to seek support from HR in getting my group that space. We used a lot of external vendors, such as printing companies, paper vendors, photographers, etc., and were constantly visited by their representatives. We argued that being in the lobby level of the building it would be easier to control the movement of these external vendors. They would not be wandering around corporate work areas where they might stumble on to something the company felt was proprietary. Because so many new people were moving into Corporate Headquarters, and we were a relatively small group, the powers that be said, "Sure, let the graphic designers have the lobby level space." What a break! We were four floors away from the rest of the employees, all by ourselves on the lobby level. Because it was the lobby level we had an entrance where you had to ring a bell and be "buzzed in" to our area. It was private, fairly large, we had our own conference room, a large common work room, all of our special equipment, and we could be the first out in case of a fire! It was the best corporate space I ever worked in for graphic design. We finally had our own, relaxed central space. We did not feel that we were being observed all day long. We could laugh there, and we could quietly try to come up with exciting graphic design concepts and solutions. Because we were a bit isolated we didn't need to *exactly* conform to the rest of the standard office space regulations. It was possible for each designer to design his or her own work space. It was a dream. When visitors, external vendors, and our business group partners would come to our area, we greeted them in a small conference room just inside the front entrance to our space. Rarely would any visitor venture into the back of the space where each designer had his or her own work space. I know the theory that designers must be physically located right next to their business group partners. However, being distanced from them was not all bad. Designers and business group partners had more than enough opportunity to meet face-to-face every day. The elevator trip down to our department was not a very long one or really inconvenient for anyone. Designers also made the short elevator trip up to the business group floors several times a day. The difference, and it was a critical one, was that we had our own private space which nurtured creative, strategic graphic design.

Now I know what I just described is rarely possible, but if you can try to find a somewhat out-of-the-way space for your graphic design group it will go a long way toward nurturing creativity.

Rejuvenation

No one can be creative 24/7/365. Creative burn-out, even if temporary, is very common in our profession. This is especially true when a graphic design department is somewhat understaffed and each designer has several projects to deal with at any one time. Contrary to popular belief, we just do not sit down and "work our magic" at the drop of a hat. Highly creative strategic graphic design takes some time, and can be somewhat exhausting. I have never met a really talented strategic graphic designer who could be creative, non-stop, all day long. Everyone needs a little rest once in awhile. This is another instance of why I became a great believer in not dedicating graphic designers to particular product lines or business groups. By being able to vary the assignments I gave to my graphic design staff, I always took into consideration the complexity of the assignment, the time allotted to complete the project, what other projects a particular designer might have on their plate at the moment, and the particular business partner who was requesting the design project. Some business partners were more difficult to work with than others, so this became a critical consideration when assigning projects to my designers. It was important to assign projects very carefully in order to nurture each designer's creativity, and save them from severe creative burn-out,. I wanted to be sure each designer would have a little breathing space to rejuvenate.

Another technique which works very well is to find non-design activities for each graphic designer each year. Sometimes it might be the ability to attend a three- or four-day graphic design conference. Or, it might be the opportunity to participate in a professional development program or workshop. Being able to attend an industry trade show to gather competitive information was also a perk which helped graphic designers rejuvenate. Even going out with a salesperson for a day to test creative concepts, was a welcome change for many overburdened graphic designers. Giving graphic designers some variety in their assignments, and the occasional opportunity to get out of the office and not do any actual design work for a day or two became, for me, an important aspect of nurturing creativity in a corporate environment. It also meant that I, the design manager, had to devote a fair amount of my own time to managing scheduling. But in the end, it was well worth the time.

The Design Manager's Personal Style

I am not sure how many graphic design managers I have met over the years, but it has to be in the hundreds. I have noted that not all graphic design mangers use the same techniques to manage their departments.

Let's start with the worst case scenario. This is the graphic design manager who manages "up the ladder." These managers are far more interested in advancing their own careers than building a great in-house graphic design group. It would seem their primary goal is to be sure that they, the graphic design managers, personally get noticed by senior corporate executives. They are hoping for salary improvements for themselves, advancement in rank and title, and praise for running a tight ship on a shoestring budget. These managers seem to care little about nurturing creativity or professionally developing and rewarding their graphic design staffs. Great designers do not stay with a company for very long under this style and type of management. That turnover leads to a great deal of time being spent by the manager recruiting replacements and then trying to "bring new recruits up to speed quickly." None of this is very healthy for anyone.

The next type of graphic design manager that I commonly find is what I call the cautious graphic design managers. These folks abhor anything that might rock the boat. They are slow to adapt to or institute change within their departments. They are usually very nice people. They are often personally very talented in many aspects of design. They don't respond well to criticism and dislike offering criticism, even if it is constructive criticism. They avoid any kind of confrontation with either their own staff or their business partners. When a graphic design department manger has these traits, the department will most likely survive, and the work all gets done, mostly on time and on budget. The problem I see with this type of graphic design manger is that the function of graphic design in a corporation tends to remain very static. No real advances for our profession occur, and finally, creativity is not nurtured, and, in fact, it is somewhat stifled.

The very best of the in-house graphic design managers I have ever met are passionate about graphic design and the added value of design, they seek out the most creative and talented graphic designers they can find, they work tirelessly to promote graphic design as a core strategic competency in the company, and they truly nurture creativity. For the most part, these great graphic design managers are also very good strategic designers themselves. They understand what design is all about. Many do not care much at all about advancing to a higher level in the company in a non-design capacity. I might add, to do everything necessary these managers work long hours. Managing an in-house graphic design group is not a nine-to-five occupation!

As I mentioned at the beginning of this chapter, there is no one way to effectively nurture creativity. Every in-house graphic design group is somewhat different. Corporate cultures also differ. The most important thing is that a graphic design group manager continuously looks for ways to nurture creativity. An in-house corporate graphic design group that stops being creative is a group that will always remain a drop-in service center.

CHAPTER 16

Anticipating and Overcoming Obstacles

I DEALT WITH THIS ISSUE in my book "Creating the Perfect Design Brief," but it is so important to the topic of this book, I wanted to include it here as well.

As a result of teaching my approach to moving the graphic design function from a service group to a core strategic business competency, I have learned that graphic designers and graphic design managers are intimidated by what they see as insurmountable obstacles. Most people tell me that they would love to get to the point of being an equal partner, accountable, a co-owner, and a key strategic resource, but in their company culture it will never happen! There are too many obstacles. Well, sure, there will be obstacles you will encounter. There are obstacles in almost everything we do in life. But instead of wringing our hands and saying it can never work, let's see if we can address those obstacles head-on.

Unanticipated obstacles are the single most important reason why plans fail. Every graphic designer or graphic design manager who wants to create a plan for improvement for his or her function should place significant emphasis on visualizing obstacles before they arise and making strategic plans for dealing with them.

Two Kinds of Obstacles

Conventional wisdom describes two broad categories of obstacles that can get in the way of progress: personal obstacles, and environmental/technical obstacles.

Personal Obstacles

Some personal obstacles include:

- Fear of failing
- Fear of authority figures
- Fear of accountability for decision making
- Low tolerance of, or for, change
- Risk avoidance
- Lack of specific business knowledge or training
- Lack of experience
- Lack of constructive feedback and sense of support
- Lack of personal drive or ambition
- Inability to speak articulately in front of groups
- Procrastination
- Confused priorities
- Reacting—"fighting fires!"

Pretty grim list, don't you think? The fact is that everyone has some of these lacks, fears, and traits to a greater or lesser extent. It's very important to honestly recognize them in yourself, because it is possible to change or to deal with these obstacles, neutralize them, avoid them, or go around them.

But personal obstacles are difficult because overcoming them often requires you to change habitual and comfortable ways of behaving. Also, many design managers and designers never really face up to their personal quirks. Many entertain a number of misconceptions about how they are really perceived by various constituencies.

If you recall my exercise wherein I ask each participant in my seminar to make a list of how he perceives himself, and then a second list of how he knows he is perceived by others, there is always a disconnect. Human beings tend to see themselves under a different lens than others do. Therefore, it is critical to think long and hard about your personal obstacles, and then to seek feedback from others about how you come across (even though I know this is risky!).

When I was with the Gillette Company, the company hired a consultant to help group managers with just this kind of dilemma. The consultant developed a form that was circulated to all of our direct report employees, as well as to the individuals we came in contact with on a daily basis outside of our particular department. The form asked these people to answer many questions about each manager, including an area for narrative, general comments. When these forms were completed, the consultant analyzed the collective results, and then met with each group manager on a one-on-one basis to go over the results.

The identity of who had made each comment was kept in strict confidence by the consultant. Neither the results of his analysis nor the source of any specific comment was ever revealed to the company's senior management; therefore, none of this became part of anyone's employee record. The purpose was solely to provide group managers with accurate feedback about how they were being perceived by their staffs and other peers. The process was very revealing, to say the least!

At first, I was a bit frightened by the concept. I think everyone was frightened. But, the consultant was a professional with this process, and he quickly eliminated our fears. I learned that some of my behaviors and practices could be improved. It wasn't that I was some kind of miserable failure, just that I was doing some things that were getting in the way of my becoming the kind of manager I really wanted to be. The consultant offered very positive and supportive suggestions of ways in which I could overcome some of these barriers and obstacles to my success. The key would be to develop a personal plan for improvement. I really must say, this process was one of the most helpful exercises in my career. It made me pause and reconsider some of my day-to-day practices. It made me aware of places I could improve. It was also the basis for my strong belief in making personal plans.

I have suggested trying this kind of exercise to many design managers, and they have also responded favorably to the effort. A relatively simple and inexpensive way to do this is to develop your own set of questions, distribute them to your staffs and peers, and ask them to respond—anonymously, of course. This may be the quickest way to determine what your particular personal obstacles to success really are, and then to do something about these obstacles.

Environmental Obstacles

On the other hand, environmental/technical obstacles are those blocks to success that you seem to have little or no control over. They come from others in the organization, from company culture, or even from the world outside the company. The list could be very long, but the most common environmental/technical obstacles I have encountered include:

- Lack of time
- Lack of budget
- Lack of staff support
- Lack of equipment
- Business conditions/climate
- Competitive pressure or disadvantage
- Lack of adequate physical space in which to do your work
- Other people's personal obstacles

These environmental/technical obstacles, combined with your own personal obstacles, often make dreaming of any kind of improvement seem impossible.

Dealing with Obstacles

The best way to deal with an obstacle, whether personal or environmental/technical, is to face the obstacle head-on. Sit down and make a list of all of these apparent barriers to your success. Describe your personal obstacles in detail, and then list your environmental/technical obstacles. For each item on your list, ask yourself, what will happen if the obstacle remains? Who are the people, other resources, time issues, and pressures involved with this obstacle? Can this obstacle be eliminated? How? Can this obstacle be neutralized? How? Can I change or modify my plan or it's timing to get around this obstacle? How? How serious is this obstacle—really? How much time and effort is it worth to overcome this obstacle? What new behavior would help overcome this obstacle? What help could I get from others? How do I get that help? How long will it take to overcome this obstacle?

Listing your obstacles, then asking yourself these questions, will, at a minimum, help you focus on finding solutions rather than just saying, "This is awful!" The process should also help you realize exactly what is getting in the way of your success.

There are just a few things that can happen. You could eliminate the obstacle, neutralize it, go around it, or live with it! I will be the first to admit sometimes you simply have to learn to live with it. For example, I worked with a company that had experienced a devastating fire. Most of its headquarters burned to the ground. Temporary office space was found for employees in various other locations around the city while the headquarters were rebuilt. The design group lost all of its equipment and files. Work had to begin all over again on projects currently in progress. Management said that the deadlines could not be changed. This was certainly a technical obstacle that the design group was forced to live with for a time. There wasn't really much that could be done except to face the problem, work day and night, and try to get back on track.

There were a few members of the graphic design staff who wanted to mount a major effort to delay the due dates of projects underway. The graphic design manager—quite wisely—realized that this would not be a good plan. Everyone else in the company was facing the same dilemma and was working diligently to get back on schedule. For the graphic design group's members to complain that their needs were unique, and that they therefore needed special treatment, would not make them appear like business partners. It would only reinforce the idea that they were just a service group. It was very stressful for almost a year. This is an example of an obstacle that the graphic design group simply had to live with.

On the other hand, I know of another situation in which the graphic design group simply did not have adequate space to effectively accommodate their workload. Repeated pleas by the graphic design manager for more space were denied. The cost per square foot was prohibitive—at least, that is what the finance people said. The design manager changed his tack and went forward with a plan for space that emphasized *revenue generation* per square foot. The design manager was able to demonstrate that a portion of the increases in sales and market shares were directly linked to the *results* of design activity. By using this argument, the design manager was able to effectively relate revenue increases to the facilities required by the design function to generate those revenues. They got their extra space.

For personal obstacles, it will often be necessary to seek help from sources outside of the company. Most human resource departments are aware of a variety of professional development programs, which can help people improve their personal skills, behavior patterns, and abilities. I have seen hundreds of cases where design managers were able to improve their presentation skills or negotiating skills, or overcome shyness and reluctance to be proactive, by utilizing external resources to help them with these issues.

The important thing is to identify all of your real, imagined, or potential obstacles, analyze them, and develop a sound plan to deal with them. Things will never get better until *you* take some positive steps to make them better.

CHAPTER 17

Creating a Plan for Moving Forward

Assuming you are not completely satisfied with the status quo and assuming you are serious about elevating the design function in your organization to a position of core, strategic business partnership, then you will have to develop a comprehensive plan to achieve your goals. Simply wanting it or thinking about it will never work. You will need to carefully and strategically develop an action plan to get you to your objective.

You might even need to develop two plans: a personal plan for improvement for yourself, and a group plan for your graphic design staff. The techniques are really the same for both activities. Get yourself a notebook and start designing a written plan.

Step One

The very first thing to do is to determine your real, added value to the company. This should be both your personal, added value, and the value your graphic design group adds to the business. Write your value statement(s) down in the notebook.

At this point in developing an actual written plan, try adding a few more exercises to those previously mentioned techniques. Make a list of accomplishments and failures—both your personal ones, and the ones for the group. The key to learning from this exercise is to be completely honest with yourself. The discipline of writing down and reviewing your past triumphs and mistakes will help you pinpoint areas in which you need to focus or improve your management style and your group's practice. Be careful to ensure that the accomplishments on your list are meaningful to the business. Simply saying, "I/We have never missed a deadline" is not enough! People who run businesses expect, as a matter of course, that you will always be on time, on budget, and on objective. That's why they pay you in the first place. It's not really an *accomplishment*, it's a given. Rather, accomplishments have to do with activities that have made things work more effectively. Accomplishments are those things you have done that have genuinely advanced the strategic business objectives of the enterprise. Accomplishments are things that can be *measured* in one way or another.

The mistakes are also important to recognize. If something went wrong, why did it go wrong? What could you have done differently? Why didn't you?

A few years ago, I attended the DMI European Conference in Amsterdam. Among the many excellent presentations was one by an officer from the United States Army. Yes, the army! This officer was a training specialist for the army, and he described an activity that I believe should be used by design groups everywhere. At the end of a training exercise (as well as actual combat situations), all of the participants would attend a debriefing meeting. He explained that this activity had to occur immediately after the event in order for details to be fresh in every soldier's mind. They would discuss what went well and what didn't go so well. They would explore reasons for both. Why did a particular maneuver work to their advantage? What could they have done differently to make the maneuver even more successful? What unanticipated events arose? How well did they meet the challenge of these events? What mistakes were made? Why?

I believe that this technique could be very valuable for graphic design groups. Immediately upon completion (and approval) of a major graphic design project, assemble the design team and have just this kind of discussion. Be sure to include your co-owner/partner for the design brief in this meeting. Take notes and make these notes part of your ongoing action plan for improvement. Pay particular attention to those areas that did not work as well for you as you had hoped. Then, develop a plan in your notebook to ensure that your next project will address these issues adequately.

After going through this process, you should be able to clearly identify areas that will need some concentrated work, as well as the areas of strength that you need to use in articulating your added value as a core business competency.

The PAR Formula

The PAR formula has been around for decades. I really don't recall where I first learned about it, but I do know that I have used it for more than thirty years to help me sort out my various action plans for improvement. It's really very simple.

"P" stands for a *Problem* you faced that required unique action on your part. "A" is for the *Action* you took to solve the problem. "R" is for the *Results* you obtained.

Look back over the years you have been a graphic designer or graphic design manager. You can probably recall examples of actions or events of which you can be particularly proud—as well as some that didn't work out very well. The ones for which you are proud are your achievements. What is important is that these achievements summarize your current skills, your ability to solve problems, and your ability to take positive action. Some examples that may help you get started:

- You improved workflow processes and developed a successful implementation plan.
- You found meaningful ways to shorten or improve the graphic design process cycle.
- You recognized a serious problem and took positive action to fix it.
- You produced graphic design solutions that increased market share, competitive advantage, the bottom line, and so forth.

This exercise will be very meaningful to your plan for improvement. Again, by writing these things down in your notebook, you will be able to begin understanding which actions you have taken in the past that produced positive results, and which actions often led to negative results. This same process relates to the debriefing meeting I just mentioned. What problems arose, what action did you take when the problem surfaced, and what were the results or outcomes of this action? If you don't write these things down and take a hard look at the lists, you will undoubtedly never really focus on the areas in which you need to improve.

Play on your strengths, and develop a list of weaknesses that need to be addressed. Now, using a calendar, set dates—real dates—and a list of actions you will take by those dates to eliminate, or overcome, your weaknesses. The key for all of the activities I will describe is to set *dates* for actions. If you don't set realistic dates, your plan will never work. It's too easy to say, "I really have to get to that someday." You'll never do it. Trust me!

I will confess that one of my personal obstacles is that I tend to procrastinate. It is remarkably easy for me to say to myself, "I'll get to that next week." And then next week, I will find another very rational reason to put the activity off a little longer. It is best never to say to people like me, "I'll need this some time in the spring." You won't get it until midnight the first day of summer! The only way I have been able to overcome this personal obstacle is to be sure I set exact dates for completion or delivery of an action item. For me, an exact due date on my calendar forces me to plan my time effectively. I feel pretty certain that many of you are the same way.

A Master Plan Needs to Be Specific

Get hold of an organization chart and determine the role graphic design plays in each function of the company. Set dates for contacting people in those functions, and for offering to come by and have a chat with them about their graphic design needs. Plan in advance what kinds of help you are able to offer. Write all of this down in your notebook! Always relate graphic design to *their* needs and the needs of the company. Remember what John Tyson would say in a meeting: "I'm here to *invest* in your future." Never, ever, go into these kinds of meetings with a list of *your* problems or issues. "They" don't really care about your problems.

By the same token, as you develop function-by-function lists of design's uses and design needs, begin to develop a list of the individuals in each of those functions whom you need to develop mutually valuable relationships with. How will you meet them? Through a cold call? Should you get someone to introduce you? Who will that person be? As always, set real due dates for these activities—and then meet those due dates.

Getting to the "Right" People

It is critical to develop an internal network of people in your organization who can help you get visibility, credibility, and trust. But how do you find these people and make meaningful contact with them? The following suggestions will help you get started:

- Use the organization chart to get a list of names.
- Do some research to find out which of them are the actual stakeholders for graphic design issues.
- Determine whether they have had any previous experience with your graphic design function. Was it positive, or negative? Why?
- Consider what graphic design issues they will most likely be facing in the short term—and the long term.
- Find out who their mentors, friends, allies, and detractors are.
- Finally, develop a plan to meet with them.

Before your first meeting with these individuals, prepare questions that demonstrate your knowledge of both the company's business issues and their specific business issues. Ask many questions. Don't try to "sell" graphic design or the graphic design function. Rather, focus on how you can effectively partner with your colleague and contribute to his or her success. After you meet with each person for the first time, always suggest a follow-up meeting at which you can present some ideas of how graphic design can help solve some of his or her business problems, and specifically, how your graphic design group can work with him or her to solve these problems. It's also a good idea to invite him or her to visit your turf. Schedule an exact date and time for a next meeting. Don't ever simply say, "I'll get back to you." Rather, you should be saying, "I'll meet with you on [date/time] to go over a definitive plan with you." It's also a good idea to follow-up these meetings with a memo, email report, or some other written document. Above all, *nurture* these new relationships.

Obstacle Planning

Work through the list of obstacles to success you created earlier. Develop concrete plans (again, with specific dates) for overcoming these obstacles in the most effective way possible. Involve your entire staff in creating all of these plans. It really should be a group effort.

Action Plan Formatting

There are as many formats for "action plans" as there are management gurus who devise them. All of them, in my mind, are equally effective—if they work for you. The format of your personal plan is just that, personal. If it works for you, it's a good format. The important criteria to include are the specific actions you must take to reach your goals. Prioritize this list, and include completion dates for each item. Note the specific steps you will need to take to achieve each goal, and devise a way to measure progress. Above all, stick to your plan.

A few typical goals of such plans include:

- Getting the company to value you and the graphic design function
- Becoming the recognized expert in graphic design issues
- Becoming a key contributor to the business, not the "art person"
- Becoming essential to the success of the business
- Becoming a strategic business partner

I have worked with several graphic design groups that actually did take the time to create a plan for "resetting" the graphic design function in their companies, but then carefully filed the plan away when the workload got particularly heavy. Please don't do this. The development of a plan, and then adhering to that plan, is the only way to achieve your goals for the graphic design function.

It is the responsibility of the graphic design function's manager to take the leadership role in this process.

Many years ago, when I first managed a small corporate graphic design group, I believed I could not only manage the group, but also do some graphic design projects myself. At the time, it seemed to be the best of both worlds. Unfortunately, as I began to realize what it really meant to be a graphic design manager, I also had to face the reality that I would have no time to do graphic design work myself. It was a tough decision. I would venture to say that all of the really great, successful graphic design managers I have known over the years faced the same realization. A graphic design manager must have the time to manage and lead. This will most likely mean you won't have time to do graphic design projects yourself. It's worth giving some thought to this. If you want graphic design to be a center for excellence, a valued and trusted partner in the corporation, and a strategic contributor to the overall success of the business, then the graphic design function needs, and deserves, full-time leadership. It is a major commitment.

CHAPTER 18

A Few Final Words

As a way of summarizing the key elements included in this book, I would like to offer a few final thoughts derived from my many years of managing corporate graphic design groups, consulting with a large number of global corporations, networking and talking with a great many peer graphic design mangers, teaching seminars, presenting workshops for in-house corporate graphic design groups, and lecturing for a number of design associations.

As I mentioned at the outset, the professional training in design I received, primarily at the University of Connecticut and UCLA, prepared me well to embark on a career as a graphic designer. However, this education gave me very little insight into the ways of the great corporate world.

I spent the first five years after graduate school teaching design at a small private college. I thoroughly enjoyed my initial (short) teaching career. Teaching offered me an opportunity to settle down and rethink many of the things I had learned in my own college career. It also provided me with the opportunity to travel in the summers. I spent a great deal of time in Europe going to museums, meeting and talking with European designers, and visiting a few European design schools. All in all, that five-year investment in the teaching profession ultimately helped me immensely.

However, I reached a point where I believed that it was time to enter the corporate world and start "doing real design." To say that I immediately felt "thrown to the wolves" is an understatement! It didn't take very long to realize that what I believed I had to offer wasn't really valued that much by non-design business managers. I quickly joined the ranks of graphic designers who whined constantly about not having enough time, not having enough budget, being generally abused, and taken for granted as an "artist." I was not a happy camper! Designers suffer from a huge "whine factor"! My suggestion to designers is to "stop whining and begin to take actions to improve our profession.

Fortunately, I had a few mentors during my career who offered me some valuable guidance. It was these people who told me I needed to find a way to learn more about *business.* I was enrolled in an Executive Development Program at the University of Michigan. It was a one-year program that probably changed my life.

In the article on design management by Earl Powell, Earl described how hard he lobbied for funds for his design group staff to attend various professional development programs. Earl realized, as many of us have, that just being a graduate of a design school will never be enough. Designers in the corporate arena need to develop their managerial, leadership, and business skills—the stuff we didn't get in design school.

What has come to be known as "professional development" in the corporate world takes on several meanings, depending on your particular area(s) of responsibility. For some managers and executives, it means pursuing an MBA at an accredited business school. For others, it is participation in extended executive development programs, such as the one I attended at the University of Michigan, and which are offered by various colleges and universities worldwide as part of their extension programs. For a great many managers, it is attendance at various seminars with titles like "Training the Trainer," The Art of Negotiation," "Conducting Effective Performance Reviews," or "Accounting for Nonfinancial Managers." All of these types of programs have their merits—as well as their drawbacks.

Many managers find participation in a full-time MBA program just too strenuous when added to the already heavy demands of their jobs and their families. College or university extension executive development programs are typically easier to accommodate, since they typically are designed as a series of one-week residency programs over a course of a year or more. They do tend to be pricey, and are often scheduled at times when it is inconvenient to be out of the office for a week at a time.

The one or two-day seminars seem to be the most popular, both for price and for minimizing time spent away from the office. For all of these options, the trick is to decide which programs are best for a graphic design manager whose aim is to advance in the ranks of management. For others, their companies make the decision easier for them by mandating areas the managers need to improve in at the time of their annual performance review. Exploration of these programs should become an integral part of your personal plan. Your plan, if done the way I suggested, should reveal the priority areas that you need to focus on very clearly. So, one very important lesson from the trenches is to continually explore and participate in a variety of professional development programs.

I have been offering seminars and in-house workshops for graphic design groups for many years. In developing these seminars I spend about six months talking with graphic design mangers about their particular needs. I also do a fair amount of research. This research has helped to further crystallize my own thinking about the future of the design profession. Graphic designers and in-house corporate graphic design managers absolutely must learn to speak a new language—the language of business. I also realized how critical a tool this design brief business is, not only for executing design projects, but also, perhaps even more importantly, for changing the perception of the design function as a whole in any enterprise.

Most of us have had to fumble around for years, trying to make sense out of apparent madness. Now is the time to stop fumbling around and make some changes. Use this design brief process as a vehicle to help you make those changes quickly and efficiently.

Using the Model as a Guideline for Change

The research also led me to developing the model I outlined earlier in this book. I have been using this model for more than a decade. Although a few people have had some problems getting it to work for them, the vast majority of people who have implemented it report that within a year or so, perception of graphic design as a valued partner had increased dramatically in their organization. It really does work. But don't kid yourself—it won't work overnight.

Meaningful change always takes an investment of time. If you are not prepared to invest the time and effort necessary to effect positive and meaningful change, nothing will ever improve. You will continue to be the overworked, under-appreciated service provider.

I strongly suggest that you take the various elements of the model, one by one, to your staff meetings. You only need to set aside twenty minutes or so at each weekly meeting to discuss the various topics. Involve everyone in your graphic design group in the discussions of each element. Be sure to allow for differences of opinion among your staff. Differing opinions and perspectives lead to fruitful debate. Try the exercises, and then allow your staff to develop a group plan of action.

A Few Important Lessons I Have Learned

Lesson #1: Improve your *business* communication skills, and use the design brief process as a tool to communicate the strategic, added value of design.

Please note, I am suggesting your focus be on improving the perception of added value of graphic design as a core strategic competency. I have met many in-house graphic design managers who spend far too much time and effort trying to advance their own careers. They tend to work at making their own personal abilities stand out, hoping to draw attention to themselves as managers, rather than to draw attention to the added value of graphic design to the enterprise. If you can advance the perception of graphic design as a core, highly valued, strategic contributor to the business, trust me, your own personal stock and reputation will automatically advance as well. Having a let's-make-it-happen attitude and bottom up leadership style will bring you more respect in the corporation.

The design brief process I have described offers nearly all of the powerful opportunities really necessary to educate and persuade non-design business partners that graphic design is a core business competency that plays a major role in the success—or failure—of any business.

Lesson #2: Develop a comprehensive action plan—and follow it. Be sure there is a time line for completion of each action item, and that there are one or more members of your staff accountable for the completion of each item.

Lesson #3: Always involve your entire graphic design group in developing plans for improvement of the function. Don't try to do it all alone.

Lesson #4: When you are in a position to hire new graphic designers for your group, look at not only a candidate's portfolio, but also look at their skills in communication, persuasion, business acumen, and confidence. Hire the brightest, most talented people you can find. Be sure their temperament will work in both your group and the company as a whole. Not everyone is really suited to work in a corporate environment. Corporate environments tend to have unique cultures, politics, and yes, some restrictions. Be sure your potential new hire will be an asset to your group and not a hindrance. Take your time in hiring. Check candidates out carefully. Interview each candidate more than once. It is usually too difficult to get permission to hire new staff. Be sure you get it right each time.

Lesson #5: Actively promote on-going professional development for each person on your staff. Consider all the available options including more formalized extension courses, and professional seminars and workshops. I constantly hear, "We have so much work on our plate, I can't possibly free up time for staff to participate in professional development programs." It is critical to find a way! Not only will you have staff with more knowledge and tools to do their jobs, but you will have staff that feel valued and refreshed after being permitted to leave the office occasionally.

Lesson #6: Be sure to spend meaningful one-on-one time with each of your staff. Group meetings are fine, but most of us deeply appreciate having the opportunity to chat with our manager more personally. When these meetings occur, actively *listen* to what they are saying. This is not the time for the manager to do all the talking. Make sure that all your staff realizes that you consider each of them unique individuals. Each of your staff wants to feel valued, trusted, and respected by you, the in-house graphic design manager.

General Precepts

Finally, I'd like to offer you several of my general "precepts" which I discovered over the years. I have touched on most of these in more detail in this book:

- *Involve others in the work of the graphic design function.* This doesn't mean designing by committee but rather valuing business input from others. Know your key stakeholders and *talk* to them.
- *Be careful of the terms you use when describing graphic design activities.* You are not the "art service bureau." You don't have "clients" or "customers," you have business partners. You don't work "for" people; you work "with" people, who are your partners.
- *Get your nose into everything that has to do with the business of your company.* Read the business press to learn more about your industry. Attend major industry trade shows. Ride along with salespeople as they contact customers. Attend major sales meetings, and talk to attendees about what they are seeing in the marketplace. Visit every functional group in the company. Learn about their activities and their business issues. Determine what role graphic design plays in each function. Then become an ally, an advisor on graphic design issues for every facet of the business.
- *Understand, and then effectively communicate, the added value of graphic design to the success of the business.* Become an ally—a partner—particularly with marketing people. You will be attending to challenges they never even thought about.
- *Take your show on the road.* Leave the graphic design studio and take a tour through your business. Send pertinent graphic design articles to strategic supporters. Write a monthly or quarterly article emphasizing the value of graphic design for your internal employee newspaper or magazine. Think about producing your own "Graphic Design Quarterly" for employees. Don't emphasize beauty or cleverness; rather, emphasize business results and benefits of good graphic design.
- *Enlist the support of your CEO.* Do everything possible to ensure that the CEO is aware of your positive business contributions to the company. Invite him or her to visit your studio.

- *Research executives to raise consciousness.* It will make them part of the solution when you ask them about their issues and concerns. When they are part of the solution, they are truly your partners.
- *Create an easy-to-understand graphic design policy statement for your function.* Include strategic objectives in the policy. You will need one for credibility.
- *Get your own budget.* Potential supporters won't come to you if you are going to charge them for the privilege. You must be easy and accessible to partner with—not costly.
- *Involve your staff in every discussion.* They will feel empowered, involved, and more motivated.
- *Invest all the time that is required to achieve your goals.* Over the long term, it will actually save you time in the future.
- *Network with other graphic design professionals outside of your company.* Isolation only leads to loneliness and narrow thinking. Attend design conferences and seminars to meet with your colleagues. Keep in touch with them as you share ideas, strategies, triumphs, and failures. Learn from one another.
- *Pursue ongoing professional development opportunities.* Use your human resources group for assistance.
- *Never, ever, forget the target audience.* Know and understand the people you are designing for.
- *Always think strategically.* Become a leader, not a follower. Be proactive.

In conclusion, the single, most critical lesson is that in order for in-house graphic design to have credibility and trust in the organization, graphic designers need to learn how to think and communicate in a different way. Graphic designers need to be able to articulate the value of graphic design clearly and simply, in terms that are more about the benefits of graphic design than the design itself. They need to study the business in depth, and to determine the roles of all kinds of graphic design activity in that business. They also need to proactively develop partnerships and alliances throughout the organization in order to get the support and trust they so desperately want. Finally, graphic design needs to be a true strategic business partner throughout the organization, working *with* people, not *for* people. It is possible to bring design out of the "trenches" and onto the organization's main playing field, but it is up to the graphic design profession to make this transition on its own.

About the Author

PETER L. PHILLIPS
Design Management Strategy Consultant

Peter L. Phillips is an internationally recognized expert in developing corporate design management strategies and programs. He has had more than thirty years experience as a senior corporate design manager, a consultant, an author, and a lecturer. He distinguished himself in the corporate world as Director of Corporate Design for the Gillette Company and as Director of Corporate Identity and Design for Digital Equipment Corporation. In both positions he had global responsibilities for managing strategic design functions.

Mr. Phillips's corporate career has crossed several industries. In addition to his Gillette and Digital Equipment Corporation assignments, he has been a television set designer and producer for Group "W" Westinghouse Broadcasting, Director of Promotional Program Development and Design for Stanmar Inc., a major East Coast resort developer and operator, and president of his own design management firm.

As a consultant, Peter has developed numerous global design strategy programs for many Fortune 500 companies. He also advises corporations on restructuring, and repositioning, their in-house corporate design groups.

Peter takes a highly pragmatic, business-based approach to all of his assignments, believing that design, and the management of corporate design functions, is a problem-solving discipline rather than a simple aesthetic exercise.

He has been the recipient of numerous awards and honors including the prestigious *Financial World* Gold Trophy for design of the Best Annual Report in the United States, as well as for development of promotions, promotional material design, communications, and for designing and implementing effective brand management systems.

Mr. Phillips is the author of "*Creating the Perfect Design Brief: How to Manage Design for Strategic Advantage,*" Allworth Press, 2004, second edition, 2012, as well as the Spanish, Portuguese, and Estonian language versions of this same book. He is also the author of "Principles of Managing the Corporate Design Department," a section of the anthology *AIGA Professional Practices in Graphic Design,* Allworth Press, 2008, and numerous articles for the *Design Management Journal.*

He has been a contributor to the books, *Careers by Design,* by Roz Goldfarb, Allworth Press, 2001; *Revealing the Corporation,* by John M.T. Balmer and Stephen A. Greyser, Routledge, Taylor & Francis Group, 2003; and *UX Best Practices, Processes, and Techniques: Achieving Impact with User Experience,* by Helmut Degen and Xiaowei Yuan, McGraw-Hill, 2011.

Peter Phillips has been a columnist for both *Graphis* magazine, and *New Design* magazine. The British Design Council has engaged him to create a knowledge cell and video on design briefs for their website: (www.designcouncil.org.uk/briefing)

Phillips has developed case studies on brand identity for DMI and the Harvard Business School that are being distributed by the Harvard Business School. He was a member of the former Design Management Advisory Panel for the University of Westminster (London, England) Business School. He also served on the Advisory Board and was an adjunct professor in design management for the Suffolk University Executive MBA Program in Innovation and Design Management. Phillips has served as a member, and secretary, of the board of directors of the Design Management Institute (DMI). In addition Phillips is an Honorary Director/Advisor of the Hong Kong International Jewelry Designer Association.

He founded the DMI Professional Development Program, and develops and conducts workshops for design management professionals worldwide. His workshops are offered as in-house, on-site training for corporations. Along with Professor Emeritus Stephen A. Greyser of the Harvard Business School, he is the co-developer and co-presenter of a Senior Executive Workshop program entitled *Strategies for Developing, Maintaining, and Sustaining a Powerful Brand.*

He is a frequent guest speaker for a wide variety of organizations in the United States, Europe, and Asia. Topics include: "Creating the Perfect Design Brief," "Developing and Implementing Strategic Global Design Programs," "Managing the Corporate Design Department," and "Selling Strategic Design Up the Corporate Ladder."

Mr. Phillips earned a Master of Arts Degree from the School of Fine Arts, University of California at Los Angeles, and a Bachelor of Fine Arts Degree at the University of Connecticut. He has also completed the curriculum requirements for a PhD in Fine Arts at UCLA, and has completed post-graduate studies at the University of Colorado, and the University of Michigan, School of Management.

Suggested Reading

Books

Peter L. Phillips, *Creating the Perfect Design Brief: How to Manage Design for Strategic Advantage*. 2nd ed. New York: Allworth Press, 2012.

American Institute of Graphic Arts. *AIGA Professional Practices in Graphic Design,* edited by Tad Crawford. New York: Allworth Press, 1998.

Balmer, John M.T., and Stephen A. Greyser. *Revealing the Corporation.* London: Routledge, 2003.

Borja de Mozota, Brigitte. *Design Management: Using Design to Build Brand Value and Corporate Innovation*. New York: Allworth Press, 2004.

Chajet, Clive. *Image By Design From Corporate Vision to Business Reality.* New York: McGraw-Hill, 1997.

Cohen, Alan R. and Bradford, David L. *Influence Without Authority.* New York: John Wiley & Sons, Inc., 1990.

Dreyfuss, Henry S. *Designing for People.* New York: Allworth Press, 2003.

Goldfarb, Roz. *Careers by Design.* New York: Allworth Press, 2001.

Gorman, Carma. *The Industrial Design Reader*. New York: Allworth Press, 2003.

Harrison, Allen F. and Bramson, Robert M. *The Art of Thinking.* New York: Berkley Books, 1982.

Heller, Steven, and Véronique Vienne., eds. *Citizen Designer.* New York: Allworth Press, 2003.

Koch, H. William, Jr. *Executive Success, How to Achieve It—How to Hold It.* New Jersey: Prentice-Hall, Inc., 1976.

Marsteller, William A. *Creative Management.* Chicago: Crain Books, 1981.

Kenneth R. Andrews, *The Concept of Corporate Strategy* (Homewood, Ill: Richard D. Irwin, 1987).

James Adams, *Conceptual Blockbusting* (New York: W. W. Norton & Company, Inc., 1979).

Jay Conger, *Winning 'Em Over: A New Model for Managing in the Age of Persuasion* (New York: Simon & Schuster, 1998).

Edgar H. Schein, *Organizational Culture and Leadership* (New York: Jossey-Bass Inc., 1992).

Peter Keen, *The Process Edge* (Boston: Harvard Business School Press, 1997).

Wendy Briner et al. *Project Leadership* (Hampshire, UK: Gower Publishing, 1990).

William R. Daniels, *Group Power II: A Manager's Guide to Conducting Regular Meetings* (San Diego, CA: University Associates Inc., 1990).

Periodicals

The Design Management Journal. Boston, Massachusetts: Design Management Institute Press. Published quarterly.

Graphic Design: USA. New York: Kaye Publishing. Published monthly.

Graphis. New York and Zurich: B. Martin Pedersen. Published bimonthly.

How. Cincinnati, Ohio: F&W Publications. Published bimonthly.

Notes

Chapter 1

1. Earl Powell, "Developing a Framework for Design Management," *Design Management Journal* (Summer 1998).

2. *Design Management Journal* (Summer 1998): 13

Chapter 3

3. Artemis March, "Paradoxical Leadership: A Journey with John Tyson," *Design Management Journal* (Fall 1994): 17.

Index